The Capricorn Book
Everything You Should Know About Capricorns

CRAFTED BY SKRIUWER

Copyright © 2025 by Skriuwer.

All rights reserved. No part of this book may be used or reproduced in any form whatsoever without written permission except in the case of brief quotations in critical articles or reviews.

At **Skriuwer**, we're more than just a team—we're a global community of people who love books. In Frisian, "Skriuwer" means "writer," and that's at the heart of what we do: creating and sharing books with readers worldwide. Wherever you are in the world, **Skriuwer** is here to inspire learning.

Frisian is one of the oldest languages in Europe, closely related to English and Dutch, and is spoken by about **500,000 people** in the province of **Friesland** (Fryslân), located in the northern Netherlands. It's the second official language of the Netherlands, but like many minority languages, Frisian faces the challenge of survival in a modern, globalized world.

We're using the money we earn to promote the Frisian language.

For more information, contact : **kontakt@skriuwer.com** (www.skriuwer.com)

TABLE OF CONTENTS

CHAPTER 1: INTRODUCTION TO CAPRICORN

- Basic overview of the Capricorn sign
- Why people find Capricorn interesting
  Core influences from element, ruling planet, and symbol

CHAPTER 2: THE HISTORY AND ORIGINS OF CAPRICORN

- Ancient civilizations and their role in shaping zodiac ideas
- Babylonian and Greek myths connected to Capricorn's symbol
- Influence of Saturn and winter solstice traditions

CHAPTER 3: KEY PERSONALITY TRAITS OF CAPRICORN

- Serious and logical approach to life
- Reliable and patient character
- Inner depth vs. outward calm

CHAPTER 4: CAPRICORN AT HOME AND WITH FAMILY

- Capricorn's need for order and routines
- Role within the family structure
- Balancing responsibilities and personal comfort

CHAPTER 5: CAPRICORN AND FRIENDSHIPS

- Initial caution when making new friends
- Loyal support and practical advice
- Handling conflicts and misunderstandings

CHAPTER 6: CAPRICORN IN ROMANTIC RELATIONSHIPS

- *Slow and steady approach to love*
- *Balancing emotional needs and rational thinking*
- *Long-term commitment and shared goals*

CHAPTER 7: CAPRICORN IN THE WORKPLACE

- *Methodical work ethic and organizational skills*
- *Leadership style: calm guidance*
- *Challenges: overwork and need for structure*

CHAPTER 8: COMMUNICATION HABITS OF CAPRICORN

- *Direct, careful, and concise expressions*
- *Listening quietly before offering thoughts*
- *Avoiding emotional drama, preferring logical discussions*

CHAPTER 9: EMOTIONAL CHARACTERISTICS OF CAPRICORN

- *Private yet deep emotional world*
- *Managing worry and self-criticism*
- *Importance of trust and safe outlets*

CHAPTER 10: STRENGTHS THAT HELP CAPRICORN SUCCEED

- *Dedication, patience, and practical thinking*
- *Ability to remain calm under stress*
- *Steady progress toward long-term goals*

CHAPTER 11: WEAKNESSES AND CHALLENGES FOR CAPRICORN

- *Fear of failure and overworking*
- *Stubbornness and resistance to change*
- *Struggles with showing vulnerability*

CHAPTER 12: CAPRICORN AND PHYSICAL WELL-BEING

- *Value of structured health routines*
- *Balancing rest with constant effort*
- *Practical diet and fitness approaches*

CHAPTER 13: CAPRICORN AND FINANCIAL MATTERS

- *Cautious approach to saving and spending*
- *Respect for earning money through real work*
- *Long-term financial security and planning*

CHAPTER 14: HABITS AND SELF-REFLECTION FOR CAPRICORN

- *Building daily routines and managing time*
- *Avoiding perfectionism and burnout*
- *Using self-reflection to adjust personal habits*

CHAPTER 15: CAPRICORN AND OTHER ZODIAC SIGNS

- *Comparisons with fire, earth, air, and water signs*
- *Managing differences and finding common ground*
- *Communication tips for harmony*

CHAPTER 16: CAPRICORN THROUGH DIFFERENT AGES

- *Childhood seriousness and teenage ambition*
- *Early adulthood career focus*
- *Midlife and later years: shifting priorities*

CHAPTER 17: COMMON BELIEFS AROUND CAPRICORN

- *Stereotypes about being cold or work-obsessed*
- *Historical and modern views shaping these beliefs*
- *Debunking myths through personal examples*

CHAPTER 18: CAPRICORN IN SOCIETY AND CULTURE

- *Roles in community, business, and leadership*
- *Media portrayals and public perception*
- *Contribution to stable social structures*

CHAPTER 19: NOTABLE CAPRICORN TALENTS

- *Methodical problem-solving and reliability*
- *Quality control and patience in learning*
- *Leadership through steady guidance*

CHAPTER 20: LOOKING AHEAD FOR CAPRICORN

- *Adapting to changing technology and work styles*
- *Balancing tradition with innovation*
- *Future goals: legacy, personal growth, and fulfillment*

CHAPTER 1: INTRODUCTION TO CAPRICORN

Understanding the Zodiac

People have looked at the sky for many centuries to see what the stars and planets might tell us about ourselves. There are 12 zodiac signs in astrology, and each one has certain traits that people think might shape how someone feels or acts. Capricorn is the tenth sign in the zodiac. Many believe that understanding Capricorn can help a person learn about possible strengths and weaknesses they might have. Even though some people do not trust astrology, others enjoy reading about these signs as a way to think about their own habits and choices.

Capricorn's Place in the Zodiac

The zodiac begins with Aries, moves through signs like Taurus and Gemini, and eventually reaches Capricorn near the end of the cycle. Capricorn is usually linked with the dates from around December 22 to January 19, though the exact dates can change slightly each year. Because Capricorn is close to the end of the zodiac, it is sometimes viewed as one of the more serious signs. People who are born at this time of year might share some common traits, according to astrology. These traits can include being responsible, trying to stay organized, and having a cautious approach when making decisions.

Symbol of Capricorn

The symbol often linked with Capricorn is the sea goat. This creature is not a real animal in everyday life. It looks like a goat in the top half, while its lower half looks like a fish's tail. This symbol can sound unusual, but it is meant to show that Capricorn might be connected to hard work and ambition (the goat part) as well as emotions and imagination (the fish part). The goat half can also be seen as strong and steady, climbing rocky mountains to reach the top. Meanwhile, the fish tail may remind people that Capricorn also has feelings that run deep, even if this side is not always shown on the outside.

Element and Modality

In astrology, each sign is linked to one of the four elements: fire, earth, air, or water. Capricorn is an earth sign, along with Taurus and Virgo. Earth signs are often seen as steady, careful, and practical. They might prefer steps they can predict, like saving money, making plans, and following rules that they believe will keep them safe. Capricorn is also what is called a "cardinal" sign. In astrology, this means Capricorn starts the winter season in many parts of the world. Cardinal signs are often thought to start new cycles or fresh phases, even if they do so in a quiet, cautious way.

Ruling Planet

Saturn is considered the planet linked to Capricorn. Saturn might sound serious, as it is said to represent time, discipline, and limits. Because Capricorn is ruled by Saturn, people often think that Capricorns have a sense of responsibility. They might feel more comfortable when they know what the rules are, and they could try hard to meet the goals they set for themselves. They might also be tough on themselves if things do not go as planned. Some believe that this link to Saturn makes Capricorn seem wise beyond their years, even as children.

How Capricorn Sees the World

Many times, Capricorn is linked to a practical view of life. This means a Capricorn might try to do things step by step, planning out each action. They might want to know the facts before making a choice. Being stable is often important to them. This does not mean they never have fun, but they might prefer events or pastimes that let them feel secure and calm. Because of this outlook, others sometimes think Capricorn is serious or reserved. But, underneath this calm view, Capricorn can have many hopes and creative ideas.

Common Traits

Some people say Capricorns are dependable and steady. They might be the friend or family member who shows up on time and keeps their word. They also might take a long time before choosing their path. This careful thinking can come from not wanting to make mistakes. Capricorns may not like taking risks that feel unsafe. They could take on tasks one by one, but they keep going even when it is hard. This makes them appear determined. Sometimes, this need to be steady can make Capricorns a little stubborn, but it can also help them finish tasks that others might abandon.

Why Capricorn Is Interesting

Many people notice Capricorn because of the balance between its outer strength and its inner depth. On the outside, Capricorn might look like a person who follows the rules and stays on a reliable schedule. Yet, on the inside, a Capricorn might have big dreams, powerful emotions, or a strong drive to do well. This mix can make Capricorn interesting to watch. It also can mean that a Capricorn might take a while to trust others with their feelings, as they prefer to keep certain thoughts to themselves until they feel safe.

Typical Capricorn Goals

Many Capricorns are known for wanting to do well at tasks that matter to them. They might focus on their studies or their job, aiming to reach a high level of skill. This could mean reading books that teach them new things, or practicing a craft until they are confident. They might save money for a safe future, or they might keep track of tasks on a list to stay organized. Setting goals, whether small or large, may give Capricorn a sense of direction. These goals often deal with things like work, relationships, or personal growth.

Capricorn in Everyday Life

You might have a Capricorn friend who shows up with the right supplies at a group event, just because they thought ahead. Another Capricorn might be the one who keeps a calendar of birthdays, so they never forget to call someone. Still another might be the child in class who prefers to sit quietly and listen, only talking when they are sure of the answer. In daily life, Capricorns often bring a sense of calm, structure, and responsibility. This might make them the people who clean up after a party or who make sure everyone around them is safe and content.

Positive Sides of Capricorn

Being trustworthy, loyal, and patient can make a Capricorn a reliable friend or family member. They often keep secrets, so if you tell them something private, they usually do not share it with others. Also, they tend to work hard at the things they care about. Because of this, they might get respect from teachers, bosses, or friends. They do not always speak loudly about what they are doing, but they keep going, step by step, until they reach the results they want. Their steady style can inspire others to stay strong during tough times.

Challenges for Capricorn

While there are many good things about having a strong sense of responsibility, it can also lead to stress. A Capricorn might worry if they cannot do everything perfectly, or they might feel bad if they have to skip an event because they have tasks to finish. They might also be too hard on themselves, feeling like they need to be perfect. Sometimes, they also might seem a bit distant, because they do not show their feelings too soon. This can make it hard for people around them to see that they have a warm side too.

Capricorn's Quiet Side

Even though Capricorns can hold strong opinions, they might not always share them. They could remain calm or quiet in a group, only speaking if they feel they have something meaningful to say. Because of this calm front, others might think they do not have many feelings. Yet, Capricorns do feel a lot on the inside. They just might not say everything out loud until they feel it is the right time.

Reason for Capricorn's Strong Sense of Goals

For some Capricorns, feeling stable is very important. They want to make sure they and their loved ones are safe. They might think that reaching their goals will help them achieve stability. This is why they can seem so driven to move forward in certain areas of life. If they want to learn a sport, they might do daily practice. If they want to build a business, they might read about financial rules. This steady approach can help them reach far, though it might also bring worries about not doing enough.

Views on Friendships and Relationships

Capricorn is known for being loyal. When they like someone, they might stick with that person through ups and downs. They often prefer close friendships with people who are also responsible or understanding. They might not be drawn to friendships that feel chaotic or unpredictable. This does not mean they never enjoy fun or silly times, but they prefer to know where they stand in a relationship. As a result, they might take a while to open up, but once they do, they can be very caring.

Capricorn's Link to Earthy Energy

As an earth sign, Capricorn is grounded and practical. This can mean they are good at seeing what is needed in a real-world situation. They might not be interested in wild ideas that seem impossible to carry out. Instead, they might ask questions about how, when, and why something will work. This can make them great problem-solvers. They can see the steps needed to fix a problem, and they might take action when others are unsure how to start.

Common Misunderstandings

A big misunderstanding is that Capricorn cannot enjoy simple fun because they are always working or planning. In truth, Capricorns can enjoy many kinds of activities, but they might be choosy about what they do and who they do it with. Another misunderstanding is that Capricorns do not care about feelings. This is not true. They might just need to feel safe before they show emotions. It is also sometimes said that Capricorns cannot be creative. Actually, they can be quite creative, especially when they see a purpose for their ideas.

Capricorn and Personal Values

Values are the things a person holds dear. For Capricorn, values might include honesty, hard work, and loyalty. A Capricorn might avoid actions that feel dishonest or reckless. They might also prefer to spend time around people who share these values or at least respect them. If someone breaks a Capricorn's trust, it can be hard for the Capricorn to trust that person again. Because of this, some Capricorns keep a smaller circle of close friends. They want to feel sure that those people respect their values.

Why Learn About Capricorn?

Many people find it helpful to read about their zodiac sign. It can offer ideas about why they might act or react in certain ways. It can also give hints on how to handle stress or how to make smarter choices. Even if a person does not fully believe in astrology, the ideas linked to Capricorn might still be helpful. They might think, "I do like to feel safe," or, "I am careful with my money," or, "I feel better if I have a plan." These ideas can help them understand themselves better.

Setting the Stage for More Detail

This chapter has shared the basic idea of what Capricorn is in astrology. It touched on the date range, the symbol of the sea goat, the element of earth, and the ruling planet Saturn. It also explained that Capricorn is often seen as steady, responsible, and sometimes a bit reserved. This foundation can help us look closer at other sides of Capricorn in the chapters ahead. The next chapters will explore more about how Capricorn came to be, historical beliefs about it, deeper personality traits, and other parts of life that might connect to this sign.

Closing Thoughts

Capricorn holds a special place in the zodiac as a sign linked to structure, care, and dependability. It is ruled by the serious planet Saturn, but that does not mean Capricorns cannot smile or laugh. Their symbol, the sea goat, shows that there is more than one side to Capricorn. There is the goat that climbs steadily, but also the fish tail that holds a deep and emotional side. By getting to know Capricorn better, we might learn that being careful, steady, and strong can be balanced with having dreams and feelings as well.

CHAPTER 2: THE HISTORY AND ORIGINS OF CAPRICORN

Ancient Civilizations and the Zodiac

Long before modern times, many groups of people made charts of the stars. They noticed that certain groups of stars seemed to stay in the same shape, and they named these shapes after animals, people, or objects. Different civilizations had different names for these star clusters. Over time, the ancient Babylonians, Egyptians, Greeks, and Romans each had their own stories about the stars. They saw patterns in how the sun seemed to move through these constellations during the year. This was how they started linking periods of time to certain signs, such as Capricorn.

Babylonian Traces

The Babylonians are often credited with early forms of astrology. They lived in an area called Mesopotamia thousands of years ago. They used the stars to mark times of year, to plan harvests, and to try to predict events. In their lists of constellations, they recognized something similar to the sea goat. Over time, this shape or symbol came to be seen as Capricorn in later civilizations. The Babylonians were interested in how the heavens could offer signs about people's future, so they began to write down these ideas.

Greek Myths and the Sea Goat

The ancient Greeks had many myths about gods and strange creatures. One myth says that the sea goat could be linked to a god named Pan, who had a goat's horns and sometimes the lower body of a goat. In some stories, Pan jumped into a river to escape a terrible monster, which changed part of him into a fish. Another story might link Capricorn to the goat Amalthea, who cared for the infant Zeus.

Myths varied over time, but all of these tales gave shape to the idea of a creature that was part goat and part fish.

Symbol of the Sea Goat

The sea goat symbol itself has been around for a very long time. It is sometimes seen in ancient artwork. In Babylonian works, a creature called the "goat-fish" appeared. People who studied these old artifacts believe that this creature could bring luck or protection. Over time, Greek and Roman astronomers matched it to a constellation in the sky. When the Romans named the zodiac signs, they kept this shape as Capricorn, from Latin words meaning "horned goat." Even though the idea of a sea goat might seem odd, it was common in many ancient stories.

Capricorn in Roman Times

During the Roman Empire, astrology became popular. Wealthy Romans might pay experts who studied the stars to learn about the best times to start projects or to hold important events. Capricorn, as the tenth sign, was linked to the winter solstice in the Northern Hemisphere. This was an important time of year when the days were short and the nights were long. Romans believed that this was a time for careful thought. Some also linked Saturn (the ruling planet of Capricorn) to agriculture in earlier times, though by Roman days Saturn also stood for discipline and limits.

Why the Winter Solstice Matters

In many parts of the world, the period around December 22 is one of the darkest times of the year. After this point, the days slowly become longer. This period was special to many ancient people. They saw that nature was quiet and the weather could be harsh. It was a time to store food and take care of important tasks indoors. In astrology, this moment was linked to Capricorn, which was seen as a sign of caution and strength. Because of the darkness, people had to be resourceful and patient, two traits often linked to Capricorn.

Influence of Saturn in Myths

Saturn has a long history in myths. In Greek stories, Kronos (the Greek name for Saturn) was a titan who was often linked to time. In Roman culture, Saturn was sometimes honored as a god of agriculture in older tales. The link between Saturn and Capricorn suggests that this sign has something to do with the passage of time, lessons, or serious thinking. Astrologers took these old myths and combined them with what they observed in the sky to shape the traits that we now associate with Capricorn.

Capricorn in Ancient Astrology Texts

Old astrology books often note that Capricorn people might act older than they are, as if they feel the weight of Saturn. This sense of maturity was thought to come from the idea that Saturn rules over time and that the winter solstice was a serious season. Ancient astrologers wrote that Capricorn often brought a focus on duty and on what one could achieve through hard work. They also mentioned that this sign might feel a push to take charge or guide others, because it was an earth sign that liked to see real results.

Changing Ideas Over the Centuries

As centuries passed, astrology changed. Different cultures shared stories and star maps, and new ideas were added. Capricorn stayed connected to the sea goat, to the winter solstice, and to Saturn. But the details of what that meant could differ. Some texts focused on the cautious and patient side of Capricorn, while others might have shown it as a sign that values success and respect. Even today, modern astrology websites might say slightly different things about Capricorn, but many keep the same broad themes that trace back to ancient times.

Why These Myths Still Matter

You might wonder why people still talk about myths and old ideas in today's world. One reason is that stories about the stars can be fun and can show how ancient people explained their world. Another reason is that these myths shaped the astrological system that many people still follow. Even if someone does not fully believe in astrology, they might still find it interesting that a sign like Capricorn has roots going back thousands of years. By knowing these stories, we can see how the sign got its symbol and why certain traits have been linked to it.

Capricorn Across Different Cultures

While Babylonian, Greek, and Roman stories are some of the most well-known sources of Western astrology, other regions also tracked the stars. In China, for example, there is a system with 12 animals for each year, not month. The Chinese zodiac does not use Capricorn, but some people have tried to compare Western astrology and Chinese astrology to find parallels. In India, there is Vedic astrology, which also studies the positions of planets. Though the approaches differ, sometimes the sign that matches Capricorn in Western astrology can share certain ideas, like being steady or careful.

Link to Mountain Goats

The idea of a goat climbing high up on rocky peaks has often been used as a symbol of ambition. Since ancient times, people have watched goats in mountainous regions walk sure-footed on steep cliffs. This image reminded them of a person who can keep going, even when the path is tough. Capricorn's link to a goat might have grown stronger because of how goats look determined and ready to scale great heights. Adding the fish tail was a reminder that there is also a part of Capricorn that can handle emotional depths.

Star Positions in the Sky

Astronomically, Capricorn is a constellation that might not be the brightest. It can be a bit harder to see in the night sky compared to some other constellations, like Orion. Still, it is visible in certain months of the year, and star charts show the shape that is said to look like a goat or a triangle. Because it was in the sky during a time of darkness in ancient lands, it could have seemed mysterious or powerful. This was another reason it drew people's attention.

Naming the Constellation

The word "Capricorn" comes from the Latin "Capricornus," which roughly means "horned goat." Over time, people shortened "Capricornus" to Capricorn. Some older texts might say Capricornus, while modern writings usually say Capricorn. Either way, both names refer to the same zodiac sign and constellation. The shape in the sky is not as clear as some star patterns, but the name stuck, and so did the idea of a partly goat and partly fish creature.

Impact on Astrology's Growth

Capricorn played a role in how people viewed astrology because it was part of the 12-sign cycle. Ancient astrologers wrote about it in detail, noting that it began at the winter solstice. This made it an important marker in the yearly calendar. They saw it as a sign of endings and new beginnings, because after the shortest day of the year, the sun would slowly bring more daylight. In some cultures, this led to the sign being linked with slow growth, or a quiet but steady push toward a new season.

Differences Between Old and Modern Views

Ancient times did not have as much scientific knowledge about space as we have today. They relied on observation, myth, and tradition. Modern astrology still borrows from these old ideas, but it has also added ideas from psychology and self-help. For example, older texts might describe Capricorn mainly in terms of good or bad luck, while modern ideas might talk about Capricorn's mindset or ways to cope with stress. Even so, the core symbol and element remain, linking modern Capricorns to their ancient roots.

Capricorn's Link to Mythical Themes

Because Capricorn involves a creature that is both land-based (a goat) and water-based (a fish), it can be seen as bridging different worlds. Some myths talk about creatures that can move between the sea and the mountains. This might have suggested that a Capricorn can be strong in real-world matters (the goat side) while also having the ability to feel deep emotions (the fish side). Ancient storytellers often enjoyed these half-and-half creatures because they added a layer of mystery to their tales.

Historical Beliefs About Capricorn's People

Ancient astrologers wrote that those born under Capricorn were often resourceful, because they were linked to the start of winter. People had to be practical to survive cold months and plan for the rest of the year. They might be watchful, not rushing into anything. They could also be patient and used to waiting for the right time to act. These ideas matched what people saw in nature: winter is a time of rest for the land, leading to renewed activity when spring arrives. Over time, these observations turned into the personality traits we see described for Capricorn.

How History Shapes Our Current View

Knowing the history of Capricorn can help us see that these traits did not appear out of nowhere. They came from stories, from close looks at the stars, and from the needs of people living during harsh winters. Modern life might be different, but the main ideas about being strong, careful, and determined stayed the same. Today, when someone reads about Capricorn, they are connecting with an old line of thought that stretches back across many cultures.

CHAPTER 3: KEY PERSONALITY TRAITS OF CAPRICORN

Looking Beneath the Surface

Some people see Capricorn as strict or distant. But there is more to Capricorn than just being cautious. When a person takes time to watch how a Capricorn acts, they might notice gentle qualities and a kind heart. These traits might not show up right away because Capricorn usually needs time before sharing them. They may prefer a quiet entrance rather than showing off. Still, many notice that Capricorns are steady and thorough in their thoughts and actions.

Serious and Thoughtful

One of the most common things people say about Capricorn is that they can be serious. This does not mean they never smile or enjoy fun things. It means they might look at life in a careful way. They can be the type of person who stops to think before jumping into something new. They value safety and order, so they do not like rushing. They often ask questions such as, "Is this a good idea?" or "Will this help me reach a real goal?" By doing this, they try to avoid problems that can come from hasty decisions.

Organized and Prepared

Many Capricorns keep a daily planner or use a schedule to be sure they know what is happening each day. They like knowing what tasks they need to complete and how they can finish them in a timely way. This sense of order helps them feel calm. Some might keep a tidy room or work area, while others have a specific way of sorting papers or other items. When a Capricorn feels overwhelmed, they might make a list of steps to get things back under control. Being organized helps them avoid confusion.

Hard-Working and Persistent

If you ask friends or family members to describe a Capricorn, they might say "They do not give up easily." This is because Capricorns usually stick to a plan until they see results. They are not afraid of steady effort. In fact, they often prefer taking one careful step at a time. They might choose the safest path instead of the quickest one, but they will keep going until they get where they want to be. This quality can help them succeed in many parts of life, including school, sports, hobbies, and future jobs.

Logical and Clear-Minded

When looking at a problem, a Capricorn often likes to see the facts. They want to know the details so they can decide the best way to solve the issue. This does not mean they never use their feelings; it simply means they enjoy proof. They might ask for clear explanations or step-by-step directions. Because of this, they can be strong at tasks that need logic, like making budgets or planning a project. They might enjoy puzzles where they can reason out the solution, rather than guessing.

Ambitious and Goal-Focused

A Capricorn often sets goals for the future. Sometimes these goals are related to learning, like getting good grades or mastering an art skill. Other times, they might relate to personal growth, such as becoming more patient or saving money for something meaningful. A Capricorn likes the idea of improving over time. They do not always talk about their plans, but they take pride in moving closer to their targets. This can make them feel confident and ready to take on new tasks.

Respectful of Rules

Capricorns are known for liking rules and guidelines. They might feel safer when they know what is allowed and what is not. They might follow instructions in school or at work closely, because that helps them get things done the right way. However, this does not mean they cannot think outside the box. They just want to be sure they are doing things in a way that keeps them and others secure. They may also notice when other people break the rules, and this can bother them. They might see fairness as very important.

Self-Reliant and Independent

Many Capricorns enjoy doing things on their own if they can. They like to prove to themselves (and sometimes to others) that they can handle challenges. They might choose a task that some see as hard and try to master it through practice. If someone offers too much help, a Capricorn might feel as if they are losing control of the process. They do not mind teamwork, but they prefer to know that they can stand on their own two feet if they need to.

Careful Decision-Making

When facing a big decision, a Capricorn often weighs all sides. They think about what might happen if they choose option A or option B. This can be good because it stops them from rushing. On the other hand, it might make them feel anxious if they think too long. They can get stuck in their thoughts, wondering which path is best. Still, once they make a decision, they often stand by it. They trust the careful thinking they used to get there.

Calm Under Pressure

In a crisis or a high-stress moment, a Capricorn might keep a level head. Others could panic, but Capricorn may keep things under control by looking for clear steps to fix the problem. This does not mean they do not feel worried inside. They often do, but they try to manage that worry by staying practical. Their focus on problem-solving can help them guide others toward safety or a solution. Later on, they might feel tired from the stress, but in the moment, they hold their composure.

Private About Feelings

Some people might think Capricorns do not have strong emotions. This is not true. They simply do not show their feelings to everyone. They might need a long time to trust someone before opening up. If they feel hurt, they may remain quiet and try to deal with it themselves. This can cause misunderstandings if friends or family think Capricorn is cold or uninterested. In reality, Capricorn can feel very deeply. They may just prefer to share those feelings in small, private moments with people they trust.

Patient Listeners

A Capricorn friend can be a good listener because they want to understand a problem fully before giving advice. They might not speak up right away, but they are taking in all the details. Then, when they do speak, they might offer thoughtful suggestions based on what they heard. They do not usually enjoy talking just for the sake of talking. They want their words to be meaningful. Because of this, others might go to Capricorn when they need a caring ear and a calm outlook.

Reliability in Teams

Even though Capricorn likes independence, they can be a dependable member of a team. In group projects at school or group tasks at work, a Capricorn usually takes on their share of the effort. They try not to let others down. They often show up on time and do what they promised to do. People might count on them for tasks that need focus. Because of this trust, Capricorns might be asked to lead certain parts of a project or handle important details.

Respect for Tradition

Capricorn can have a deep respect for customs or established ways of doing things. They might take part in events that have been done the same way for years, as long as those events feel important and safe to them. They like the security that comes from knowing the steps of a process. This is not because they lack creativity, but because they see value in methods that have worked well in the past. They might also enjoy learning about history or old techniques that are still useful today.

Sense of Self-Discipline

Many Capricorns have a strong sense of what they should or should not do. They might put rules on themselves, like getting homework done before watching a show. They do not always need someone else pushing them because they push themselves. This self-discipline can help them reach their goals. However, it can also be stressful if they become too strict with themselves. If they fail at something they planned, they might feel extra disappointed, even if others do not see it as a big mistake.

Possible Tendency to Overwork

Because Capricorns like to reach goals, they can sometimes take on too much. They might want to prove their value by doing all their tasks without a break. While this drive can help them accomplish a lot, it might also lead to stress. They could forget to rest, which can cause tiredness or frustration. Learning to set limits and take care of themselves is important for them. They have to remember that rest is not the same as being lazy.

Polite but Strong Views

Capricorns do have opinions. They might not always show them, but inside, they have their own sense of what is right and wrong. When they do speak up, they can be clear about why they believe something. They might use facts or results to back up their views.

This calm style can help them in debates or arguments. They might stay polite, but they do not easily give up on what they think is correct. Others might find this firmness both impressive and a bit intimidating.

Problem-Solving Mindset

One of Capricorn's gifts is spotting what might go wrong before it happens. They can look ahead and notice possible dangers or issues. While some might see this as worrying, it can be helpful for planning. For example, if they are on a team building a project, they might say, "We need an extra tool, in case the first one breaks." This foresight might save everyone from trouble later. Capricorns thrive in areas where steady thinking is required, such as planning events or managing resources.

Preference for Quality Over Quantity

When choosing what clothes to buy, what friends to trust, or how to spend their time, Capricorns often focus on quality. They might prefer one sturdy pair of shoes over many cheap ones. They might have a small circle of close friends rather than a large group of acquaintances. This is linked to their cautious nature. They want to invest their time and energy in things or people who will last. This approach can help them avoid feeling overwhelmed, but it also means they may seem picky to others.

Inner Resilience

Because Capricorns do not always show every emotion, they often develop a type of inner strength. When problems arise, they might think, "I can handle this," even if they feel tense. They might take a quiet moment to collect their thoughts and figure out a plan. This resilience can keep them going in tough situations. Over time, they might gain a reputation for being strong or unshakable. Even if they do feel afraid, they try not to let that fear stop them from carrying out their tasks.

Ability to Adapt, Slowly but Surely

While Capricorn might not enjoy change as much as some signs, they can still adapt. They just do it in steps. For instance, if they move to a new place or change to a new school, they will look for ways to bring order into the new situation. They might set up their space in a neat way or look for safe routines. Bit by bit, they find a way to handle the new environment. This patient, steady approach can help them feel comfortable over time, even when life shifts.

Keeping Secrets

Because they are private themselves, Capricorns often respect other people's secrets. If a friend confides something important, they usually do not share it with others. They know how it feels to keep personal thoughts hidden, so they do not want to break that trust. This can make them a safe friend for people who need someone who can listen without gossiping. It also shows how important honesty is to them.

Seeking Self-Improvement

Even though Capricorn might appear confident or reserved, they often think about how they can do better. They might read books on areas they want to improve or ask for advice from someone they trust. This desire to improve does not come from wanting to show off. Rather, they want to feel prepared for the future. They might learn new skills or try different methods to see if they can handle tasks more smoothly. They enjoy feeling they have grown in areas that matter to them.

Resisting Too Much Attention

A Capricorn typically does not want a lot of attention or praise from a huge crowd. They often prefer that people notice their work quietly, without a big fuss. If someone compliments them, they might say, "I was just doing what needed to be done." They might not do well with too much spotlight. Instead, a simple acknowledgment from a person they respect can mean a lot to them. Though they like recognition for their efforts, they might feel shy or uncomfortable when many people focus on them.

How These Traits Form a Whole

When we look at each of these qualities, we see that Capricorn's personality has many layers. They can be strong and quiet, serious but also caring, very organized yet sometimes flexible in small ways. They are comfortable with plans but can handle surprises when they must. All these traits together create a person who tries to bring a sense of steadiness wherever they go. They might not be the loudest or the quickest in a group, but they often act with purpose.

Why Understanding These Traits Matters

Learning about these traits can help friends, family, or teachers see why a Capricorn acts the way they do. If a Capricorn friend is slow to share feelings, it might not be personal. It could just be part of how they protect themselves. If a teacher sees a Capricorn student asking many questions, the student might simply be trying to be sure they do the work correctly. By understanding these traits, people can support each other in a better way.

Keeping Balance

While these qualities can be helpful, it is also good to remember that everyone needs balance. A Capricorn's need for control or order can sometimes stop them from trying something new. A bit of risk can lead to growth, too. On the other hand, the calm and careful style of Capricorn can inspire friends who might be more impulsive. Each of these traits can be powerful if used with care. Learning when to apply them and when to loosen up can help a Capricorn feel well-rounded.

CHAPTER 4: CAPRICORN AT HOME AND WITH FAMILY

What Home Means to Capricorn

Home can be a special place for Capricorn. It is where they feel safe and can act like themselves without worry. In this space, they can set the rules they like, keep things neat, or find comfort in calm surroundings. The idea of having a secure base is important to them. They might prefer homes that are well-organized, where family members follow a regular plan. This does not mean the home must be fancy. Rather, Capricorn prefers a place that feels stable and welcoming.

Role as a Family Member

In many families, the Capricorn child or teenager might be the one who makes sure everyone is on time. They might remind others about chores or tasks. As adults, Capricorns may become the planners of family events, making sure every detail is handled. Because they enjoy feeling prepared, they might keep track of birthdays, schedules, and other important dates, so things do not slip by. Their loved ones often depend on them for that sense of order.

Tidy Spaces and Routines

Some Capricorns like their spaces to be neat. They might have a certain spot for each thing, such as a special area for shoes or books. This helps them find what they need quickly. If the house gets messy, they might feel stressed until it is fixed. They often prefer routines like having meals at the same time each day or following a certain plan in the morning. This can make the home feel calm, which is important to Capricorn's well-being.

Family Traditions and Shared Activities

Capricorns can hold dear the customs or shared times that bring the family together, especially if those practices have been around for a while. For instance, if the family has a habit of having a big meal on a certain day or telling stories at night, Capricorn might help keep that going. They appreciate the feeling of belonging that comes from sharing simple acts as a family. Because they enjoy structure, they might try to make these special times run smoothly, perhaps by doing tasks ahead of time or preparing items the family needs.

Communication at Home

At home, Capricorn might be quieter than some other signs. They might not talk about their day until they feel it is the right time. When they do share, they focus on the main points and facts, rather than using lots of extra words. If there is a problem, a Capricorn in the family might try to fix it calmly. Sometimes, others might wish Capricorn would be more open about their worries or hopes. Still, Capricorns usually show they care through actions, like helping cook a meal or doing chores without being asked.

Supporting Siblings

If Capricorn has brothers or sisters, they might take on a helpful or guiding role in the family. They might be the one who teaches a younger sibling how to do a difficult task or helps them with homework. They often think ahead, so they might warn a younger sibling about what could go wrong if rules are not followed. This can come across as strict, but it usually comes from a caring place. Capricorns do not like to see their siblings get into trouble or make the same mistakes they have seen before.

Handling Family Conflicts

Every family faces disagreements sometimes. Capricorns often want to solve problems in a mature way. They might suggest taking a break to cool down and then talking about a fair solution. They do not enjoy shouting matches, and they prefer an approach that helps everyone feel heard. If a conflict cannot be solved immediately, a Capricorn might feel uneasy. They might think about it a lot, looking for ways to bring balance back. This sense of responsibility can weigh on them, so they might need support from other family members as well.

Practical Help Around the House

Many Capricorns enjoy doing practical tasks that help the household. This might be fixing broken items, cleaning up, or organizing the pantry. They feel good when they see the results of their work. They also like feeling useful. If another family member is not as interested in these chores, Capricorn might quietly take on extra tasks. However, they could grow resentful if they feel they are carrying too much of the load alone. They need to remember to speak up and share tasks with others.

Privacy and Quiet Time

Even in a full house, Capricorn may seek out a private corner for themselves. They might need time to read, think, or rest without noise. This helps them process their thoughts, which can get crowded if they are always around people. Family members who see a Capricorn teen or adult spending time alone should understand that this is normal for Capricorn. They might simply recharge their energy by being in a calm space. They are not ignoring loved ones; they just need that mental break.

Handling Changes at Home

Life changes might include moving to a new place, welcoming a new family member, or adjusting to a new schedule. These events can be stressful for Capricorn, who prefers familiar surroundings. They might show their stress by becoming extra neat or even more quiet than usual. They might try to make lists of everything that needs to be done. Over time, they can adapt, but they need patience from others. Letting Capricorn help plan the details can make them feel more in control and less nervous about the unknown.

Being a Support to Older Relatives

As Capricorns grow older, they might show a strong sense of duty toward parents or grandparents. They might visit them often, handle chores for them, or help them manage important papers. They might see it as their role to ensure that older relatives are safe and have what they need. If a Capricorn is a young person, they might lend a hand by carrying groceries or doing yard work for an older family member. Feeling helpful and dependable can give them a sense of purpose.

Teaching Responsibility to Younger Generations

In a family with younger children, Capricorn might help teach them basic tasks like cleaning up or setting the table. They might do this by creating a simple chart or routine. Because of their knack for organization, they can be good at showing the steps needed for each chore. They might also explain why these tasks matter for the well-being of the whole family. Sometimes, younger kids might find this guidance strict, but in the long run, it can help them learn valuable life skills.

Encouraging a Stable Home Atmosphere

Capricorns often work quietly to keep the home steady. They might avoid bringing drama or chaos into the house. If they sense tension, they might take action to calm everyone, maybe by making a plan to solve the issue. Their steady presence can help family members feel secure. This does not mean they ignore problems, but they do not want fights to get out of control. A Capricorn might prefer small group discussions or one-on-one chats to large emotional confrontations.

Sharing Practical Wisdom

If a family member is confused about money, schedules, or planning for the future, Capricorn can offer ideas based on logic. For instance, they might show a sibling how to manage an allowance or how to break a big project into smaller parts. They might also share tips on how to keep a clean room without getting overwhelmed. Because they love order, they usually have a system for everything, from how they fold clothes to how they organize a study desk. Sometimes, they just need to remember that not everyone has the same approach, so they must stay patient.

Bonding Through Quiet Activities

While some families might go out for loud and lively gatherings, Capricorns can often bond with loved ones through quieter pastimes. This might be reading together, playing board games, or watching a show as a group. They are usually content with activities that let them relax in a safe environment. That does not mean they never try exciting things, but they generally like to do them with planning. At home, they often enjoy simple, cozy pastimes that do not create too much of a mess.

Challenges in Expressing Feelings

Sometimes, family members might want a Capricorn to share more about what is going on inside their mind. Capricorns can find it difficult to put all their emotions into words. If a parent or sibling asks, "How do you feel about this?" they might just get a short answer. One reason is that Capricorns want to solve feelings on their own. Another reason is that they can be afraid of sounding silly or weak. Over time, learning to share small pieces of their inner world can help their family understand them better.

Responsibility in a Parenting Role

Later in life, when a Capricorn becomes a parent, they might take that role very seriously. They could be the type of parent who makes sure their child is well-fed, properly clothed, and always on time for school. They value teaching good manners and practical skills. However, they might also have to watch out for putting too many rules in place. Striking a balance between structure and freedom is often a goal they must work toward.

Dealing with Finances at Home

Capricorns often pay attention to money matters in the family. If they are old enough to manage finances, they might make budgets or ensure bills are paid on time. They might also try to save for future goals. They like feeling that the household is secure, and having stable finances helps with that. In a family setting, they might advise others on spending habits or ways to avoid debt. They see this as being responsible, not just controlling.

Staying Close to Family Over Time

Some Capricorns keep tight connections with relatives even when they grow older and move out. They might schedule visits or phone calls, offering help where needed. They see their family as part of their foundation, so they do not cut ties easily. If someone in the family needs help, a Capricorn might show up with practical solutions or moral support. They believe in the idea of being there for loved ones, especially in tough times.

Respecting Personal Boundaries

Because they value their own privacy, Capricorns also tend to respect the private space of others. For example, if a sibling wants to keep something secret, a Capricorn is less likely to pry. They know the importance of trust. However, if they sense real danger in a situation, they might speak up. In those cases, they will share their concerns in a calm manner, because they do not want to see their loved ones get hurt.

Encouraging Self-Reliance in the Family

In a family with a Capricorn, others might learn to be more responsible, simply by observing how Capricorn handles tasks. Capricorns often show that people can solve problems by breaking them down. If a younger sibling or family member always runs for help, Capricorn might gently push them to try a solution on their own first. This approach can build confidence in the entire family. Over time, relatives might respect the Capricorn for teaching them how to handle challenges.

Emotional Support in Subtle Ways

Capricorn might not always say, "I love you," a hundred times a day. But they often show love by taking care of details that others ignore. Maybe they quietly fix a squeaky door so it will not bother someone at night. Or they might notice that the fridge is running low on milk and buy more without being asked. These small actions can speak volumes about how they feel. Recognizing these subtle forms of support can help others see that Capricorn truly cares.

Balancing Work and Home

Sometimes, a Capricorn can become so focused on outside duties or jobs that they spend less time with family. They might feel they have to work extra hard to provide security. While this is understandable, it can cause them to miss out on bonding moments. Finding a balance between responsibilities and family time is key. Loved ones can remind Capricorn that sharing a meal or talking about the day is also an important part of a stable home.

Celebrating Each Other's Milestones

Though Capricorn does not like big crowds or loud events, they still enjoy marking important moments for family members in calm ways. They might organize a simple get-together or buy a thoughtful gift that shows they paid attention to someone's needs. They do not have to make it flashy. They just want their loved ones to feel remembered and appreciated. For a Capricorn, the focus is on meaningful gestures that bring the family closer.

Encouraging Harmony

A Capricorn at home often likes a gentle atmosphere. They might play soft music or keep the lights at a comfortable level. They dislike fights or loud conflicts, so they may do small things to set a relaxing mood. This could include lighting scented candles or cleaning common spaces so everyone can enjoy a clutter-free area. By doing this, Capricorn tries to encourage a sense of peace that everyone can share.

Respect for Family Hierarchies

If the family has clear roles, such as parents, grandparents, or older siblings, a Capricorn might show extra respect to those in charge. They value wisdom that comes with age or experience. This does not mean they follow blindly, but they tend to listen to advice from elders before making their own decisions. They might also follow traditions passed down through the generations, as long as those traditions fit their values of practicality and security.

Teaching Through Actions

Because Capricorns often prefer "show, don't tell," they might teach lessons at home by example. For instance, if they want their younger siblings to learn about saving money, they might keep a jar where they place spare coins. Over time, they can show how that jar's contents add up to something useful. This quiet teaching style can be quite effective. It also shows that Capricorn values real results more than fancy speeches.

CHAPTER 5: CAPRICORN AND FRIENDSHIPS

How Capricorns Approach Friendship

Capricorns often look for friends they can trust for the long term. They do not always rush to make a lot of friends right away. Instead, they may focus on a few people who seem kind, reliable, and thoughtful. Having a small circle can help Capricorns feel comfortable. They can take time to understand each person's personality before they get close. Because of this, they might seem a bit slow to open up, but it is just their way of making sure they form sturdy bonds.

First Steps in Making Friends

When Capricorns first meet someone new, they often remain polite and watchful. They tend to notice small details, like how the other person acts in a group or how they handle a problem. If the new acquaintance is respectful and calm, Capricorn might start to open up more. If a Capricorn senses that the other person likes drama or does not care about rules, they might hold back. This is not because they think they are better, but rather that they value smooth, steady connections.

Qualities Capricorns Value in Friends

Honesty is usually at the top of the list for Capricorn. They do not like lies or secrets that hurt people. They also like friends who have goals or at least show some sense of direction. They do not need all their friends to share the same interests, but they do enjoy being around people who are responsible in their own way. Respecting boundaries is also very important. Since Capricorns can be private, a friend who gives them space when they need it will earn their trust faster.

Capricorn's Loyal Side
Once a Capricorn decides someone is a true friend, they often stand by them through hard times. If a friend has trouble at school, Capricorn might offer to help with homework or provide a quiet place to study. If a friend is going through emotional struggles, Capricorn may offer practical ideas to handle the issue. They might not be overly expressive with hugs or big displays, but they will show up when it matters. This steady form of caring can make them a friend people rely on.

Handling Group Situations
In a larger group of friends, Capricorns might appear quieter. They often prefer to let others do more of the talking unless the topic is something they find interesting or important. They watch how people interact, noticing who is honest and who might be spreading gossip. If the conversation turns chaotic, Capricorn might try to steer it back toward a calmer discussion. They prefer a peaceful setting where no one is being left out or teased.

Planning Group Activities
Because Capricorns are organized, they might end up planning group outings or small events with their friends. For example, if a group wants to play board games, the Capricorn might suggest a schedule, decide who brings snacks, and set a time to begin. They do not usually force others to follow every little detail, but they feel better when there is a structure. Friends might appreciate Capricorn for cutting down on confusion, especially if they do not like last-minute changes.

Dealing with Disagreements Among Friends

In any circle of friends, disagreements will happen. Capricorns usually try to solve these arguments fairly. They might ask each person to explain their side, then look for a way to make peace. They do not like shouting matches or random blame. If the disagreement involves values that Capricorn cares about deeply (like honesty), they may speak up firmly. They might say, "Let's talk it out calmly," or "We should figure out a fair solution." They often bring a level-headed approach to help the group find common ground.

Being a Dependable Friend

A Capricorn friend often does what they promise. If they say they will be somewhere at a certain time, they try hard not to be late. If they volunteer to help with a group project, they will do their share thoroughly. This dependability makes them a good friend to work with at school or in other group tasks. Their willingness to handle responsibilities can set a good example for others, although it might also lead to them carrying more weight if their friends do not step up.

Capricorn's Sense of Humor

Even though they might appear serious, Capricorns can have a dry or clever sense of humor around close friends. They might tease gently or make subtle jokes that catch people off-guard. Not everyone sees this side right away because Capricorns pick their moments. In a small, trusted group, they can let loose a bit more and show that they do enjoy laughter. Friends who appreciate a quieter, thoughtful style of humor will get along well with them.

Friendship Over the Long Term

Many Capricorns try to keep their close friendships for many years. They value the history and shared experiences they gather with someone over time. Even if life changes or people move away, Capricorn might stay in contact with a friend who was loyal in the past. This can mean regular messages or calls to keep that bond going. As they grow older, they might cherish these friendships even more because they represent trust built over many shared moments.

Giving Advice to Friends

A Capricorn friend may be good at giving practical advice. If a friend is confused about how to approach a problem, Capricorn might break it down into smaller steps. They might also suggest being patient and doing one task at a time. However, they might sometimes forget that not everyone handles problems the same way. A Capricorn might think, "This is the most sensible solution," and not realize the friend needs emotional support more than a step-by-step plan. Finding a balance between practical advice and emotional care can be a learning process for them.

Respecting Boundaries in Friendship

Just as Capricorns like their own space, they try to give friends space too. If a friend needs some alone time, Capricorn might not be offended. They understand the value of privacy. However, if a friend becomes distant without explanation, Capricorn might worry they did something wrong. They can sometimes take it personally if they are left in the dark. Talking openly can help avoid misunderstandings. Capricorns generally want to maintain steady connections rather than guess about a friend's feelings.

Friendship Challenges

One challenge is that Capricorns can come across as too strict or serious. Some people might think they do not like to relax. Another challenge is that Capricorns might struggle to connect with friends who live a very free-flowing lifestyle without plans or rules. While they do not want everyone to be exactly like them, they may find it stressful if a friend is constantly late or breaks promises. They have to learn to accept that different personalities have different ways of doing things.

Handling Friend Betrayal

If a friend breaks Capricorn's trust, it can be tough for Capricorn to forgive and forget. Because they value loyalty so much, a betrayal might hurt them deeply. They might become distant or end the friendship if the betrayal goes against their core values. Even if the friend apologizes, Capricorn might keep a careful watch to see if the friend's actions match their words. Rebuilding trust can be slow, but it is possible if the friend truly changes and respects Capricorn's boundaries.

Capricorn as a Peacemaker

In a group of friends, a Capricorn can sometimes act as a calm voice in the middle of strong emotions. They look at the facts and try to remind people of what matters most. They might say, "We are all friends. Let's find a fair solution." However, they will step away if they think the conflict is full of drama that cannot be solved in a fair way. They do not like to waste time on circles of blame. Instead, they prefer real solutions where everyone learns something.

Shared Activities

Capricorns might enjoy doing things with their friends that have a clear purpose. For example, they might like helping out at an event, going to a museum, or learning a new skill as a group. They also can enjoy quieter social moments like having a simple meal together or watching a favorite show. They do not always need loud parties to have a good time. In fact, they might feel more relaxed in smaller gatherings where they can talk calmly.

Capricorn's Circle of Trust

Over time, Capricorns build a close-knit group of people they trust fully. These might be childhood friends, classmates, or coworkers who proved their loyalty. Inside this circle, Capricorn can be more open, showing emotions they keep hidden from the outside world. They might share their worries, dreams, or deeper thoughts. Friends in this circle usually feel honored that Capricorn trusts them, because it is not easy to gain that level of closeness.

Supporting Friends' Goals

Capricorns are often supportive when a friend has an important goal, such as starting a new hobby or applying for a special program. They might help by offering tips, looking up resources, or just cheering them on in a calm, steady way. They know how important it is to have people believe in you. If the friend faces a setback, Capricorn might encourage them to keep going. They may remind their friend of the importance of patience and steady effort.

Learning to Accept Spontaneity

Sometimes, Capricorns need to learn how to go along with sudden plans. Their friends might say, "Let's do this fun thing right now!" and Capricorn might feel uneasy without a plan. Over time, they can learn to loosen up, especially when they trust the friends who invite them. They might discover new forms of enjoyment by stepping outside their comfort zone. Still, they may keep one foot on the ground in case they need to handle unexpected problems.

When Capricorn Needs Help

Capricorns tend to be givers in friendship, often taking on the role of helper or problem-solver. But there can be times when they need help too. They may not always ask for it, worried about looking weak. True friends can notice the signs that Capricorn is stressed—maybe they become more silent or distant than usual. If a friend offers kind words or practical support, Capricorn might slowly learn that it is okay to lean on others. This can deepen the bond because it shows that friendship goes both ways.

Building Friendships with Different Personalities

Capricorns can be friends with outgoing or lively people if there is mutual respect. They might enjoy the energy these friends bring, as long as they do not feel forced into constant chaos. They can also get along well with other quiet, thoughtful people who share a liking for calm settings. The key is respect for each other's boundaries and ways of living. As long as the friend's lifestyle does not clash with Capricorn's need for stability, they can find common ground.

Balancing Friendship and Alone Time

Because Capricorns need quiet moments to recharge, they might limit how often they go out. They may say no to some plans if they have had a busy week. True friends will understand that Capricorn is not rejecting them, but rather looking after their own well-being. This balance helps Capricorn stay mentally and physically healthy. It also allows them to show up fully for their friends when they do spend time together.

Mending a Broken Friendship

Sometimes, even the best friendships go through rough patches. If Capricorn wants to mend a broken bond, they might try a calm conversation to discuss what went wrong. They will likely want clear answers and steps on how to prevent the same conflict in the future. If both sides are willing to work on it, Capricorn can be patient and steady in restoring trust. If not, they might accept that the friendship cannot go back to how it was, though this acceptance can be painful.

Friendship in Online Spaces

In today's world, friends do not always have to be face-to-face. Some Capricorns might find online groups that share their interests, such as a discussion forum about a favorite hobby. They might enjoy these spaces because they can think carefully before posting, rather than having to come up with fast responses in person. Still, they will want to feel that the group follows certain respectful rules. If the online space becomes full of fights or rude comments, Capricorn might leave.

Encouraging Others to Grow

When a Capricorn sees a friend struggling with time management or other challenges, they might offer gentle tips or show them a new system. They are not doing this to be bossy. They simply see a way to help. If the friend appreciates it, this can bring them closer. However, if the friend feels lectured, Capricorn might need to pull back and let them learn on their own. It is important for Capricorn to remember that not everyone wants practical advice all the time.

Signs of a Lasting Friendship

A lasting friendship with Capricorn might include inside jokes that took shape over time, reliable help during tough events, and shared respect for each other's personal choices. Both friends know they can count on each other, even if they do not talk daily. Capricorn values these deeper bonds, knowing that true friends are not just about fun times but also about steady support. Over the years, such friendships can bring comfort and a sense of belonging.

Capricorn's Quiet Encouragement

Sometimes, a friend might be unsure about taking a big step, like applying to a new school or starting a craft they have always wanted to try. Capricorn can encourage them in a simple but powerful way, by asking logical questions: "What do you need to begin?" or "How can you schedule your time?" This practical nudge can make the friend feel more confident. Capricorn often believes that with patience and a plan, many goals are possible.

CHAPTER 6: CAPRICORN IN ROMANTIC RELATIONSHIPS

A Serious Approach to Love

In romantic matters, Capricorns are often careful and thoughtful. They do not usually rush headlong into love at first sight. Instead, they may get to know someone step by step before expressing deeper feelings. They want a stable bond, so they need to feel sure about a person's character. This can make them appear cautious, but it also helps them avoid heartbreak from poorly chosen relationships.

Traits Capricorn Looks for in a Partner

Honesty is high on the list. Capricorns want someone they can trust fully, as they do not like secrets or sudden surprises in love. They also appreciate a partner who has goals or is at least working toward something meaningful. A partner's kindness, reliability, and willingness to respect boundaries can stand out to a Capricorn. They do not need someone who is exactly the same as them, but shared values can make the bond stronger.

Getting to Know Each Other

In the early stages, Capricorn might want to spend time doing calm activities to see how the other person behaves. They might prefer a quiet dinner or a walk in the park rather than a big party. During these moments, they ask questions to learn about the person's habits, likes, and background. They pay attention to small signs of respect, such as showing up on time or listening attentively. If they see traits that match their own sense of reliability, they grow more open.

Building Trust Slowly

Trust is huge for Capricorn in romance. They might test the waters by sharing small personal details and seeing how the partner reacts. If the partner is respectful and gentle, Capricorn might share more over time. But if the partner laughs at Capricorn's worries or betrays their trust, Capricorn can close up again. Because they want something lasting, they check for signs that the person is genuine. This process might feel slow, but it helps Capricorn feel safe.

Showing Affection

Capricorns may not always show affection in loud or flashy ways. Instead, they might do practical tasks to make their partner's life easier. They could help fix something that is broken, plan a small trip (making sure all details are in place), or cook a favorite meal. They might also offer steady emotional support by listening carefully and suggesting solutions. If their partner can see these actions as signs of care, they will notice that Capricorn is trying to show love in a calm, steady manner.

Communication Styles

In romantic relationships, Capricorns typically like clear and direct communication. They prefer addressing issues as soon as possible, rather than letting them become bigger problems. If their partner avoids talking about problems, Capricorn might feel uneasy. They believe in facing difficulties with a plan. At times, they might not express all their own feelings easily, but they do want to understand their partner's thoughts. A simple, honest chat can help them feel closer.

Respecting Boundaries in Love

Capricorn will usually respect their partner's space and independence. They do not like to push or nag if the partner needs some alone time. They also expect the same respect for their own privacy. If a partner becomes too clingy or tries to control them,

Capricorn might feel trapped and pull away. They believe love should not involve breaking personal limits. Both sides should be able to keep their sense of self while sharing a strong connection.

Providing Stability

One of Capricorn's strengths is creating a feeling of security for their partner. They might help organize shared finances if they are in a serious adult relationship. They could plan routines that keep life running smoothly, like making sure bills are paid on time or meals are prepared. This practicality can be comforting. A Capricorn often feels proud when they can be a steady shoulder for their partner to lean on.

Challenges in Capricorn's Love Life

Because they can be so cautious, Capricorns might miss chances to connect with potential partners who are more spontaneous. They might also seem distant or not very emotional, causing misunderstandings. Some partners might want more open displays of feelings and wonder if Capricorn truly cares. Capricorns may need to learn ways to share their emotions more freely. This does not mean changing who they are, but finding methods to let their partner know they are valued.

Overthinking and Worrying

Capricorns can sometimes overthink a romantic situation, fearing they will make a wrong choice. They might weigh every little detail, wondering if the relationship is headed in the right direction. While caution can be good, too much can lead to stress or hold them back from enjoying the moment. A partner who can gently reassure Capricorn might help them feel less anxious about making mistakes.

Handling Conflicts with a Partner

When conflicts arise, Capricorn usually wants to solve them in a logical way. They might say, "Let's figure out what caused this argument and find a solution." If their partner is very emotional, Capricorn can feel overwhelmed or unsure how to handle sudden bursts of feeling. Taking a short break to think can help. Afterward, Capricorn tries to discuss the issue calmly. They might apologize if they see they are at fault, but they also expect their partner to own their part of the problem.

Dealing with Heartbreak

If a relationship ends, Capricorns can take it very hard because they invest so much once they trust someone. They might retreat and spend a lot of time reflecting on what went wrong. However, over time, their natural sense of responsibility kicks in, and they try to learn lessons from the breakup. They might think, "How can I avoid this kind of hurt in the future?" or "What did I do that caused problems?" They might close their heart for a while, being more careful before they open up again.

Capricorn and Romantic Surprises

Some partners might want big surprises or grand gestures. This can be tricky for Capricorn, who likes to plan everything. They can be thoughtful when it comes to small details, but they might not always think of dramatic ways to show love. If a partner wants something fancy, Capricorn may try, as long as it makes sense to them and does not break their sense of order. Learning to meet in the middle can help both sides feel satisfied.

Long-Term Commitments

Capricorns often think about the future and want a partner who does too. If they see a relationship going well, they may discuss long-term plans, like living arrangements, financial goals, or whether to have a family someday. This can happen once they feel sure about the partner's loyalty. They do not jump into serious steps without thinking. They want to know that both people share the same general hopes. This practical talk can feel less romantic, but it gives Capricorn the security they need.

Balancing Work and Romance

Capricorns tend to work hard. If they become very busy with a job or a big project, they might focus too much on those tasks and forget to set aside time for their partner. Their partner might feel left out or think Capricorn cares more about work than love. Finding a balance is key. Capricorns can make sure to plan special times just for their partner, even if they have to schedule it. This shows the partner they truly matter, not just the Capricorn's goals.

Showing Emotions in Private

Capricorns might be more comfortable sharing deeper emotions when they are alone with their partner. In a group setting, they could remain quiet. But in a safe space, they might open up about worries, fears, or hopes. This can be a tender side of Capricorn that few people see. A partner who is patient and understanding can make it easier for Capricorn to show these softer feelings. Over time, the bond can become very strong because it is built on honesty and trust.

Sharing Responsibilities

In a serious adult relationship, Capricorn likes to share tasks in a fair way. They might say, "I will handle the cooking if you handle washing the dishes." Or they might split bills if both partners earn money. They believe in equality and do not want to rely entirely on someone else for important matters. However, they are also willing to shoulder extra tasks if their partner is going through a hard time. They see teamwork as essential to making the relationship run smoothly.

Capricorn's Protective Side

A Capricorn in love can become protective if they sense someone is treating their partner poorly or if there is a threat to their partner's well-being. They might calmly but firmly confront the issue or step in to help. They do not do this to control their partner, but to make sure no harm comes to someone they care about. This protective instinct can be comforting to their partner, who realizes Capricorn is serious about keeping them safe.

Shared Activities in a Relationship

Capricorns enjoy sharing activities that bring them closer to their partner in a calm way. They might like cooking a meal together, doing home projects, or learning a new skill side by side. They also might enjoy going for walks in nature or reading in the same room. Loud or chaotic outings can be fun once in a while, but they might prefer balanced, predictable ways to connect. A partner who appreciates these quieter moments can have a meaningful time with Capricorn.

Compliments and Affection

Capricorns may not be used to giving out lots of compliments. However, when they do praise their partner, it is usually honest and thoughtful. For instance, they might say, "You put a lot of effort into that project, and it turned out great." They also like hearing that their own efforts are noticed. If their partner thanks them for something practical, like fixing a problem or being consistent, it can mean a lot to them. They might give subtle signs of affection, like a gentle touch or a soft smile, instead of big displays.

Handling Jealousy or Doubt

If Capricorn gets jealous, it usually means they sense a threat to the security of the relationship. They might try to solve it by talking with their partner in a direct, calm manner. If the partner reassures them and acts with honesty, Capricorn can let go of the fear. If they find out their partner has not been truthful, they might withdraw and think about whether the relationship is worth saving. They do not like games or dishonesty, so they might end things if they see a pattern of lies.

Growing Together Over Time

Capricorns often see love as a process of two people building something that lasts. They might hope that both partners will develop skills and stay supportive of each other. Over time, they may want to set shared goals, like moving into a place together or starting a long-term plan. As they grow older, this focus on teamwork can make a couple very strong. However, Capricorn has to be careful not to turn the relationship into just tasks and goals, remembering to add kindness and fun.

Dealing with Outside Opinions

Some friends or relatives might say, "You are being too slow to commit," or "You are being too picky." Capricorns usually do not let outside opinions rush them. They believe they know what is right for their relationship. If they are sure about the partner and the path they are on, they will stand by their decision. They might calmly explain their reasons if asked, but they do not feel the need to prove themselves to everyone.

Encouraging a Partner's Growth

When a Capricorn sees that their partner has a dream or a skill to build, they often provide steady support. They might help with planning or offer resources. They believe success takes time and effort, and they like to see their partner move forward. If the partner faces setbacks, Capricorn can offer calm words, reminding them that small steps can lead to progress. This kind of practical support can help the partner feel seen and valued.

Keeping Romance Alive

Some partners worry that Capricorn might forget romance once they feel safe in the relationship. While Capricorns might not be overly dramatic, they can still keep romance alive. They might do small, sweet acts like leaving a thoughtful note or setting aside time for a cozy meal. They could also surprise their partner with well-planned outings or gifts that show they have been listening to what the partner enjoys. These actions might be simple, but they can be filled with genuine care.

Sharing Secrets

Over time, if Capricorn feels truly secure, they might share parts of their life story or personal dreams that few people know. This is a major sign that they trust their partner deeply. They want to feel that what they reveal will be kept safe. If the partner shows understanding and respect, it can bring them even closer. This level of honesty can build a strong base for the relationship that lasts through many challenges.

Adapting to a Partner's Style

Sometimes, Capricorn's partner might be more talkative or emotional. Capricorn can learn to be patient with these traits, even if it feels new. They may not always understand why someone needs to share feelings at length, but if they truly care, they will try to offer a listening ear. In return, they hope the partner appreciates Capricorn's steady nature. Finding a balance of emotional expression and logical thinking can help each person grow in the relationship.

CHAPTER 7: CAPRICORN IN THE WORKPLACE

General Approach to Work

Capricorns are often seen as dedicated and responsible in professional settings. They usually arrive on time, fulfill their duties, and avoid careless mistakes. They tend to feel that hard effort is the path to reliable outcomes. Because of this, they might focus on tasks and goals even when others are distracted. This attitude can make Capricorns stand out as dependable team members or leaders. They like a structured environment where each person knows what is expected. If that structure is missing, a Capricorn might try to create order on their own.

Handling Authority and Rules

Capricorns often prefer knowing who is in charge and what the rules are. They thrive when there is a clear plan for how to complete tasks. If their boss or supervisor sets clear guidelines, Capricorns will usually follow them carefully. They appreciate fairness in the chain of command, so they can grow unhappy if they notice favoritism or unfair treatment in the workplace. Sometimes, if rules conflict with what Capricorn sees as common sense, they might speak up calmly or suggest a more logical way. They do not want chaos, but they also do not want rules that make no sense.

Organizational Skills on the Job

Many Capricorns keep a notebook, planner, or spreadsheet to manage their tasks at work. They may break down large projects into smaller steps. They might also set mini-goals for themselves, checking them off one by one. This methodical approach can prevent confusion and make it easier to measure success. If deadlines are pressing, Capricorns might work longer hours or skip breaks to finish what they started. Though this can bring good results, it can also wear them out over time if they do not pace themselves.

Leadership Qualities

Capricorns can be natural leaders, though they do not always shout instructions. They often guide others through planning, resource management, and problem-solving. They tend to stay calm under stress, which can be reassuring to coworkers. When a challenge arises, Capricorns might assign tasks based on each person's strengths. They look for stable, step-by-step solutions rather than quick fixes. Because they value respect and honesty, they aim to treat team members fairly. In return, they expect team members to show responsibility and put in solid effort.

Dealing with Coworkers

In a group setting, Capricorns strive to be respectful. They may not be the most chatty or friendly at first, preferring to watch how others behave. Over time, they form strong professional relationships with people they trust. They may reach out if a coworker needs help, especially when it relates to finishing a shared assignment. They enjoy seeing tasks done properly, so they might offer advice if they notice inefficiencies. Some coworkers might appreciate this guidance, while others might feel pressured. Capricorns do not usually mean to control everything; they just want to ensure the work is done well.

Communication in the Workplace

When speaking with colleagues or managers, Capricorns usually like being direct and clear. They might provide bullet points or concise explanations instead of long talks. If a problem appears, they might suggest a practical fix right away. In meetings, they might quietly take notes, then share thoughts after everyone else has spoken.

They do not mind letting others talk first, but if they see something that needs correction, they speak up. This direct style can help keep projects moving forward.

Capricorn's Strengths at Work

- **Reliability:** They often complete tasks on time and at a good standard of quality.

- **Attention to Detail:** They try not to overlook important points, making them useful in jobs that need careful checks.

- **Persistence:** Even if a project becomes complicated, Capricorns keep working step by step.

- **Logical Thinking:** They break big problems into smaller parts and manage them one by one.

- **Resourcefulness:** They search for ways to solve issues using what is available, looking for solutions that last.

Possible Challenges

- **Overwork:** Capricorns might push themselves too far, fearing they will not meet a deadline or expectation. This can lead to burnout or stress.

- **Stubbornness:** They might believe their method is the only correct way and resist new ideas from others.

- **Strictness:** In a leadership role, they could come across as too serious, making some coworkers feel uneasy.

- **Fear of Risk:** Because they like safe, logical paths, they might avoid bold choices that could lead to innovation.

- **Difficulty Delegating:** They might think, "If I want it done right, I have to do it myself," which can create a heavy workload.

Finding Fulfillment in Different Careers

Capricorns can succeed in many fields, but they often favor roles where they can see stable progress and clear outcomes. Some might do well in finance, accounting, or roles dealing with numbers, because they are comfortable being detailed and systematic. Others might excel in management, project coordination, or jobs where planning is crucial. They can also fit into technical fields like engineering or software development, where a methodical approach is needed. Capricorns may avoid lines of work that feel too unpredictable, though some learn to adapt if they see a chance for steady growth or secure results.

Approach to Promotions and Recognition

Capricorns usually do not chase praise just for show. However, they do want their efforts noticed. If they see a path to a higher position, they will work toward it carefully, meeting every requirement. If they do not receive credit for their achievements, they can feel unappreciated. In these cases, they might become unhappy or consider leaving for a job where their contributions are valued. They do not always ask for public applause, but they need to feel respected and that their labor is worthwhile.

Balancing Teamwork and Independence

Capricorns can work well on a team, but they also enjoy tasks they can handle alone. In a group, they like roles that let them plan parts of the project. They want to ensure everyone knows who is responsible for each element. If the team is disorganized, Capricorn might take the lead or suggest a structured approach. If they see coworkers being lazy or ignoring details, they might speak up. This could cause tension if others are more relaxed, but Capricorn believes it is better to be direct than let the project fail.

Coping with Workplace Stress

Because Capricorns often hold themselves to high standards, they can feel stressed when a project runs into issues. Their first reaction is usually to work even harder, which may lead to exhaustion. Over time, they must learn that short breaks and pacing themselves can improve performance in the long run. In a busy office, they might find it helpful to step outside for fresh air or have a short moment of quiet. They also might release tension by writing a to-do list, turning chaotic thoughts into concrete plans. Sharing concerns with a trusted colleague can ease the feeling of carrying everything alone.

Professional Relationships vs. Personal Friendships

Capricorns often keep a line between their work relationships and personal friendships. They may be polite and supportive at work but not share private details about their life. Some coworkers might think Capricorn is distant, but Capricorns do this to maintain a professional environment. Over time, if they discover a coworker has similar values, they may become closer, but they typically start with caution. They believe that keeping a respectful distance helps avoid unnecessary conflict or misunderstandings on the job.

Office Politics and Gossip

Many workplaces have some level of gossip or office politics. Capricorns usually prefer to stay out of drama and keep focused on their tasks. If they notice unfair actions or hear rumors, they might collect facts before reacting. They do not like nonsense that wastes time or hurts people's reputation. If someone tries to drag them into such talk, they might politely decline or bring the conversation back to work topics. They find it better to remain professional than get tangled up in unproductive chatter.

Motivating Others in the Workplace

In leadership positions, Capricorns might encourage team members through practical support. For example, they could organize tasks in a clear way so people do not feel overwhelmed. They might offer step-by-step guidance or share useful tips. Sometimes they praise a job well done, but often they show appreciation by trusting a person with more responsibility. They might say, "I know you can handle this task," which can boost the person's confidence. While they may not give loud compliments, they do try to show respect and trust for those who put in genuine work.

Capricorn's View on Workplace Ethics

Most Capricorns take professional ethics seriously. They do not like cheating, lying, or shortcuts that break the rules. They prefer honest methods that hold up over time. If they see unethical behavior, they might speak to a manager or handle it in a calm, firm way. They believe maintaining integrity not only keeps them proud of their work but also prevents bigger problems later. People who try to deceive or cut corners might annoy Capricorn, who thinks these actions damage the team's progress and morale.

Dealing with Disappointment at Work

Even with good planning, tasks do not always end well. When Capricorns face disappointment—like not receiving a promotion or seeing a project fail—they might take it hard at first. They could become quiet, replaying the events in their mind to see what went wrong. After that period, they usually shift to a more practical approach: "How can I avoid this mistake next time?" They might come back with a detailed plan for improvement, showing their strong desire to learn and do better in the future.

Work-Life Harmony

Capricorns, due to their sense of responsibility, might carry work home. They could read emails after hours or think about tasks even when they are supposed to relax. Balancing personal life and work can be a challenge. They may need to set rules like not checking messages at night or scheduling time for hobbies and rest. Once they see that personal well-being can help them work better, they become more open to setting limits. Still, it takes effort for them to let go of that sense of duty and truly unwind.

Approach to Mentoring or Training

When guiding new employees, Capricorns might break down tasks into clear instructions. They like to show step-by-step methods, sharing tips they have learned through experience. They try to be patient, but they do expect trainees to keep up and show genuine effort. If a trainee does not show interest in learning, Capricorn may become frustrated. However, if the person is eager and respects the process, Capricorn can be a steady, encouraging teacher.

Strengthening Career Paths

Capricorns often have long-term aims for their professional life. They might pick positions that give them the chance to grow over time. Each role becomes a stepping stone toward a more stable or higher-level place. They might carefully manage their reputation by being known as someone who always does their part. This helps them get positive references for future opportunities. If they find a workplace that aligns with their values, they might stay there and climb the ladder steadily. If not, they might look for a company that recognizes their diligent style.

Working Under Pressure

In high-pressure environments, Capricorns can remain calm when many others panic. They focus on immediate steps, organizing tasks so the group does not get overwhelmed. Their strong sense of duty can help them push through tight deadlines or complex issues. However, they must watch out for the signs of burnout. They might not notice they are exhausted until they have headaches or trouble sleeping. Learning to step back, delegate tasks, and trust others is part of building a healthier relationship with work.

Creative Sides at Work

People sometimes assume Capricorns do not have creative ideas, but that is not true. They can think up fresh solutions if they see a need. However, they typically mix creativity with logic. For example, if they want to change how the office organizes data, they might devise a new system that is both original and structured. They do not seek flashy methods, but they do enjoy improving things. They just like to make sure those improvements can be carried out well.

Adapting to New Technology or Methods

Change can make Capricorns uneasy if it feels sudden or poorly explained. But if someone shows them how the new technology or process can improve results, they can adapt. They often do their own research, reading instructions or testing methods on a small scale before fully committing. Over time, they can become strong adopters of updates as long as those changes make logical sense. They see the value in staying modern, especially if it helps them and their team stay competitive.

Handling Different Personalities

Every workplace has a mix of personalities. Capricorns might work alongside very outspoken people or very relaxed ones. They try to stay polite and find ways to cooperate. If someone is too unpredictable, Capricorn might keep interactions to a minimum, focusing on the tasks at hand. They recognize that diversity can help the team see different viewpoints, but they also believe in maintaining clear goals. They will help build unity by reminding everyone of the shared aim and the steps needed to meet it.

Setting Personal Boundaries at Work

Capricorns typically do not want to carry personal conflicts into the workplace. If they had a bad morning at home, they might hide it while they do their job. Likewise, they try not to let coworker arguments follow them after hours. They may see the workplace as an area for professional behavior. If someone tries to cross lines by prying into their personal business, they might respond politely but firmly. This sense of boundary helps them remain consistent and efficient.

Staying Motivated Over the Long Term

In a lengthy career, motivation can rise and fall. Capricorns keep themselves motivated by setting new objectives. For instance, they might aim to learn a new tool or gain a certification that boosts their value at work. They also might track milestones, such as finishing projects or earning positive feedback. This record of accomplishments keeps them aware of how far they have come. If they feel stuck, they might talk with a mentor or trusted colleague to find new approaches. They believe in persistent growth, as long as it is realistic and steady.

Interacting with Clients or Customers

If Capricorns deal with clients, they typically present themselves in a calm, polite way. They want the client to see them as trustworthy. They might keep track of all client requests in detailed notes, so they can deliver exactly what is promised. If a client is upset, Capricorn tries to solve the root problem rather than just smoothing things over. This might mean apologizing when necessary, then suggesting specific changes to fix the issue. Clients often appreciate this thoroughness, seeing that Capricorn genuinely wants to meet their needs.

CHAPTER 8: COMMUNICATION HABITS OF CAPRICORN

Overall Communication Style

Capricorns often speak in a direct, thoughtful manner. They do not usually waste words on small talk or casual chatter, unless they see a reason to engage. This does not mean they are unfriendly, but they tend to get to the point. Their style can be described as careful, structured, and somewhat reserved. They want their message to be clear, and they are not always comfortable with loud or overly emotional exchanges.

Preference for Clarity

Capricorns like having details in order. When someone speaks too vaguely, Capricorns might ask follow-up questions to clarify. They prefer hearing the specifics of a story rather than just a general idea. If they are the ones giving instructions, they make sure everything is laid out step by step. This helps others avoid confusion. Sometimes people who like to jump from topic to topic might see Capricorn's approach as strict, but Capricorns see it as a way to keep everyone on the same page.

Listening Skills

While Capricorns may not speak the most in a group, they are often strong listeners. They pay attention to each word, storing information so they can form a response that fits the situation. By doing this, they can offer relevant input or solutions. However, if the conversation turns into gossip or random banter, Capricorn might tune out. They value purposeful talk, where they can either learn something or solve a problem.

Tone and Word Choice

Capricorns often use a calm and steady tone. They do not usually shout or use exaggerated expressions. Instead, they rely on logic and straightforward language. Some might say they can sound serious, but that seriousness often helps them be understood. They avoid flowery or dramatic words, preferring a clean and direct way of speaking. If they are excited about something, they might show it through a slight change in pitch or by using a few more positive words, but they usually remain composed.

Body Language

When talking face to face, Capricorns might have a still posture. They might keep their arms at their sides or folded on a table, listening intently. They often look a person in the eye when they speak, which shows focus. If they feel uncomfortable, they might shift slightly or glance away, but they usually try to keep a calm expression. A subtle nod can indicate they are tracking the conversation. They are not typically the type to wave their arms or move a lot while talking, preferring a steadier style.

Expressing Feelings

Capricorns can be cautious about showing deep emotions through words. If they are upset, they might give shorter replies or speak in a cooler tone, but they may not say, "I am very angry." Instead, they express anger or frustration by pointing out what caused the problem and suggesting a fix. When they are happy, they might give a small smile or a nod of approval rather than jumping with excitement. This reserved manner can confuse people who expect big outward reactions.

Handling Arguments

In a conflict, Capricorn tries to stay logical. They might lay out facts or examples to show their point of view. If the other person starts shouting, Capricorn might step back or speak more softly, hoping to calm the situation. They want to find real solutions, not just trade blame. However, if a person continues to argue without reason, Capricorn might grow silent or walk away, thinking there is no point in continuing. They believe in fair and clear communication, so they do not enjoy loud clashes that solve nothing.

Problem-Solving Discussions

When there is a problem to solve, Capricorns like to break it down. They might say, "Let's list out the possible causes," or "What are our best options to fix this?" They rely on step-by-step reasoning, which can make them good at group planning sessions. They also want everyone to stay on topic and avoid wandering into unrelated conversations. Their direct approach can help keep the team focused, although some might find it a bit strict if they prefer a more relaxed discussion.

Talking in Groups vs. One-on-One

In a big group, Capricorn might speak up only when they have something important to add. They do not enjoy shouting over others. If the group setting feels too loud or disorganized, they might wait until it is quieter or talk to a key person privately afterward. In one-on-one talks, they can be more open, especially if they trust the other person. They appreciate the chance to share thoughts in a calm setting where they will not be interrupted.

Digital Communication

Many Capricorns use texts, emails, or messaging apps in a straightforward way. They often write with proper spelling and grammar, even in casual messages. They do not usually fill their texts with extra emojis or playful language unless they are with someone they know well. In work emails or formal notes, they keep a clear structure, such as stating the main purpose, adding details, and finishing with a polite conclusion. They see digital communication as another tool to get tasks done or share plans.

Humor and Sarcasm

Capricorns can have a dry or understated sense of humor. They might make a clever remark or a soft tease, smiling slightly as they speak. Not everyone catches on right away because the tone remains calm. They do not normally enjoy harsh or mean jokes. If the group is laughing loudly at something they find rude, Capricorn might remain quiet or politely smile, not really joining in. They prefer humor that does not cause harm or embarrassment to others.

Encouraging Others to Speak

When Capricorns have authority in a meeting, they might encourage quieter folks to share ideas, because they know how it feels to be reserved. They could say, "We have not heard your thoughts yet. Do you want to add something?" This encourages a balanced exchange. If someone is shy or worried about being judged, Capricorn might gently guide them by asking specific questions. They see value in hearing from everyone, as it can lead to a well-rounded solution.

Communicating Boundaries

Capricorns typically believe in healthy limits. If someone is pushing them too hard or invading their personal space, they might politely say something like, "I need some time to think about that," or "Let us talk about this another day." They do not enjoy hurting feelings, but they also do not like ignoring their own needs. If a person keeps pushing after a boundary is set, Capricorn might become firm or distant, showing that they will not budge on certain matters.

Sharing Personal Stories

In casual talk, Capricorns might keep stories about themselves short. They are not always comfortable being the center of attention. Instead, they might let others chat about their interests, and they chime in when they have knowledge to share. If someone specifically asks about Capricorn's life, they might give a brief overview. Only with close friends or family do they go into deeper stories or strong emotions. Even then, they pick their words carefully.

Patience and Timing

Capricorns prefer conversations where each person gets a turn to speak. They do not like when people interrupt or jump in without letting them finish. If they experience frequent interruptions, they might lose interest in the conversation or become quieter. They appreciate those who wait until they are done talking before responding. In return, Capricorns try not to speak over others and may take a breath or pause to make room for others to join in.

Respect for Different Views

Capricorns do not mind if others have ideas that clash with theirs, as long as the conversation stays reasonable. They may say, "I see your point, but here is another angle," rather than saying the other person is wrong. They aim for a calm debate based on facts or experience. However, if the other person is disrespectful or refuses to consider any new idea, Capricorn might just end the discussion. They do not see value in shouting matches or constant bickering.

Supporting Someone in Need

If someone comes to them with a personal issue, Capricorns listen closely. They might ask clarifying questions: "Have you tried this?" or "What do you think might help?" They often respond with practical suggestions rather than purely emotional comfort. While this can be very helpful in solving a problem, sometimes the person may just want an empathetic ear. Capricorns can learn to provide both logical tips and gentle understanding to make the other person feel heard.

Communicating Under Stress

When they are stressed, Capricorns might become quieter, focusing on the tension they feel. They might show shortness in their responses or seem extra serious. If someone pressures them further, they could respond with brief remarks, trying to keep emotions under control. Later, when they have had time to think, they may talk about the issue in a calmer way. They prefer to handle complicated feelings in private rather than in a group setting.

Being Persuasive

Capricorns can be persuasive by using facts, examples, or past results. If they want to convince someone to follow a plan, they might point out the practical benefits or highlight proven successes. Their calm approach can appeal to those who dislike big, flashy pitches. However, if an audience needs emotional stories or hype, Capricorn's quiet style might not land as strongly. They might adapt slightly by telling small success stories, but they generally keep to a measured tone.

Confidence vs. Modesty

Capricorns can speak confidently about topics they know well. If they have prepared or studied, they will share their points in a clear manner. On the other hand, if they feel uncertain about a subject, they might say so and remain quiet, preferring not to guess. They do not like sounding uninformed. This honesty can help them keep a good reputation for being reliable and true to their word.

Cross-Cultural Communication

In settings with people from different backgrounds, Capricorns remain respectful. They try to adapt by learning about cultural norms if needed. They might speak more slowly or use simpler phrases if language barriers exist. They are not big on forced jokes or casual remarks that might not translate well. Instead, they stick to facts and polite conversation. This approach can come across as reserved, but it often avoids confusion or offense.

Negotiation and Compromise

If they must negotiate, Capricorns come prepared with clear points about what they need and what they can offer. They do not typically rely on fancy speeches; they rely on logic and fairness. They might say, "Here is why this plan benefits both of us," then list the reasons. If the other side argues, Capricorn will weigh the new information carefully before agreeing or disagreeing. They want any agreement to be practical and workable in the long run, not just a short-term fix.

Developing Better Communication Skills

Capricorns might sometimes realize they come across as too blunt or too reserved. If they see this is causing problems, they may try to soften their delivery, perhaps by adding a friendly remark or small personal detail. They might also practice active listening, letting others know they are heard by repeating key points back. Over time, these small adjustments can help them connect better with different kinds of people.

Capricorn with Shy Individuals

When talking to someone who is very shy or nervous, Capricorns can be gentle. They might slow down the conversation, ask simpler questions, or share a calm story to break the ice. They do not push the shy person to open up immediately. Instead, they give the person space to speak on their own. If the person feels safe, they might talk more. Capricorns often respect that everyone has their own comfort level.

Capricorn with Outspoken People

In contrast, when dealing with very outspoken or loud individuals, Capricorns may quietly hold their ground. They might wait for a pause, then speak clearly. They do not want to compete in a shouting match. If the outspoken person does not give them a chance to talk, Capricorn could say, "I would like to add something," or politely indicate it is their turn. They keep a cool tone, aiming to be heard without raising their voice.

Conflict Resolution Style

If a misunderstanding happens, Capricorns prefer to meet in person or talk in a structured way to clear things up. They might say, "Let us clarify what went wrong and fix it." They do not enjoy hidden resentments or passive-aggressive comments. If the other party avoids direct communication, Capricorn might try one more time to talk things out. If nothing changes, they might accept that they have done all they can and reduce contact with that person.

Personal Growth Through Communication

Over the years, Capricorns can discover that sharing some emotions and personal stories can enhance their bonds with others. They do not have to become overly talkative, but letting people see a bit of their inner world can bring understanding and closeness. They might learn that giving a few words of praise or thanks can boost a team's spirit. By balancing their natural caution with a small dose of open warmth, they can become highly effective communicators.

Conclusion

Capricorns favor clear, measured, and logical ways of talking. They listen carefully, choose words with care, and dislike random chatter without purpose. They can appear reserved, but they often support those who need help by providing practical advice or solutions. While they might not fill conversations with lively emotion, they show sincerity by being consistent and honest. With time, they might loosen up around trusted friends, adding subtle warmth or humor. By blending their straightforward style with a bit more openness, Capricorns can maintain strong, respectful connections in many areas of life.

CHAPTER 9: EMOTIONAL CHARACTERISTICS OF CAPRICORN

Why Emotions Matter for Capricorn

Many people see Capricorn as calm and reserved. They might assume that Capricorn does not experience strong emotions. However, this is not correct. Capricorn does feel a wide range of emotions—sometimes very deeply. The difference is that they often keep these feelings inside, showing only a small portion on the surface. Understanding how Capricorn processes emotions can help friends, family, and Capricorn themselves handle emotional ups and downs more smoothly.

Inner vs. Outer World

Capricorns tend to show a calm outer face, even when they feel strong things inside. It might be fear, worry, or excitement, but they hold it tightly under control. They do this because they prefer not to let emotions rule their actions. They would rather plan ahead than act in a burst of feeling. This can be good in difficult times, as they stay steady. But it can also lead to misunderstandings if others do not realize how much is going on inside their mind and heart.

Guarded Heart

One reason for their reserved nature is that Capricorns want to avoid being hurt or embarrassed. If they open up and share everything, and the listener reacts poorly, Capricorn feels uneasy. They might think, "I should have kept that to myself." Over time, they learn to protect themselves by keeping an emotional shield. This guarded style can make them seem distant, but it also gives them time to figure out who is safe to trust with deeper feelings.

Slow to Express Feelings

Because Capricorns are cautious about sharing emotions, it may take them longer to discuss how they truly feel. If they experience heartbreak, for instance, they might bottle it up for a while, dealing with it in private. They might seem fine on the outside, going about daily tasks. In reality, they could be working through sadness or disappointment bit by bit. They do not like to rush emotional processing, preferring to think about what happened and how best to move forward.

Handling Worry and Stress

Capricorns worry about responsibilities, future plans, and outcomes. Their natural sense of duty can lead them to think about "what if" scenarios. For example, they might lie awake thinking of how to fix a family or work problem. This focus on problems can sometimes make them anxious. On the plus side, it pushes them to plan solutions. On the downside, they might not always rest enough or ask for support. They feel they should solve everything alone, which can weigh on them.

Emotional Reliability

Despite their inner worries, Capricorns are often the rock in their group. When others panic, Capricorn keeps a level head, offering logic or practical support. Their friends may notice that Capricorn rarely has emotional outbursts or sudden mood swings. Even if Capricorn does feel upset, they try not to let that emotion take over the situation. They believe in staying rational, which can be a relief for those who need a dependable presence during storms of emotion.

Fear of Failure

A key emotional driver for many Capricorns is the fear of failing at something important. This fear can push them to work extra hard. Yet it also places extra pressure on their shoulders. They might tie their sense of worth to achievements. If they miss a goal, they can feel very disappointed or upset. They might dwell on mistakes longer than other signs, replaying them to make sure it never happens again. This can be helpful for learning but painful if it becomes a cycle of self-criticism.

Pride and Sensitivity

Some might not expect Capricorns to be sensitive, but they can be. Criticism can sting deeply if it touches on a Capricorn's sense of responsibility or success. They may not show tears, but they might think about the criticism for days, trying to decide if it is fair or if they let themselves down. If the criticism seems baseless or mean, Capricorn could become quietly defensive. They may not argue loudly, but they will hold on to a sense of hurt or a desire to prove the critic wrong.

Emotional Support for Others

When someone close needs emotional support, Capricorn often helps with calm advice. They focus on practical actions to improve the situation. For instance, if a friend is very sad about a problem, Capricorn might say, "Let's see what we can do to make it better." They might write a list of solutions or research tips. While this might not be a warm hug, it can be a comforting form of help. However, sometimes people want emotional closeness more than solutions. This difference can create a gap if Capricorn does not realize it.

Deep Yet Private Feelings

Capricorns can feel love, joy, sadness, and anger as strongly as anyone else, but they often do so in private. They might cry or express frustration behind closed doors instead of in front of people.

Over time, some learn that sharing vulnerable moments with trusted loved ones builds closeness. Yet, opening up remains challenging. They might worry they will appear weak or lose respect if they show raw emotions. Balancing privacy with healthy sharing is a key emotional skill for Capricorn to develop.

Strong Sense of Guilt

If Capricorn thinks they have let someone down, they can feel guilty for a long time. They set high standards for themselves, so falling short upsets them deeply. They might replay the event and wonder how they could have done better. Apologizing can be hard because they fear admitting failure. But once they do, they truly mean it, and they strive not to repeat the mistake. Their guilt can push them to make changes, but it can also weigh them down if they do not forgive themselves after a while.

Quiet Anger

Capricorn's anger might not be loud or dramatic. Instead, it can show up as a cold or very firm response. They might say fewer words or distance themselves from the person who caused the anger. In extreme cases, if Capricorn feels truly wronged, they can cut ties. They do this to protect themselves. It might appear harsh, but for Capricorn, it is a way to keep order. If a person keeps pushing them, they may finally express anger directly, though they often try to stay civil.

Balancing Emotions with Logic

One of Capricorn's strengths is blending emotion with logic. Even when they feel strong emotions, they can pause to think about what is best in the long term. This can prevent rash actions, such as sending an angry message or making big decisions in the heat of the moment. On the other hand, there are times when pure logic is not enough to solve emotional matters, especially in relationships.

Learning to accept that some problems need open emotional exchange is important for Capricorn's growth.

Handling Positive Emotions

Joy or excitement might not show up as loud cheering from Capricorn. Instead, it may appear as a small smile, a pat on the back, or a soft glow in their expression. They might also share good news with just a few close people rather than announcing it widely. Their pleasure often comes from seeing a plan work out or achieving a meaningful goal. In those moments, they can feel a quiet but deep sense of satisfaction.

Self-Care and Emotional Health

To keep emotional balance, Capricorns can benefit from setting aside time to relax. Activities like reading, taking a gentle walk, or enjoying music can calm their busy mind. They might feel guilty for resting, but regular breaks can reduce stress. Another helpful approach is talking with someone they trust—a friend, family member, or counselor. Sharing worries in a safe space can help lighten the load. Sometimes, writing in a journal can also provide an outlet for thoughts and feelings that are hard to say out loud.

Need for Safe Outlets

Because Capricorn does not like public displays of emotion, they need safe spaces to let feelings out. This could be their bedroom, a quiet corner of a library, or any spot where they feel secure. They might express anger or sadness by writing it down, creating art, or using a calm activity to process what happened. These outlets help them avoid bottling things up until they become unmanageable. Over time, they learn that letting emotions out in a healthy way does not reduce their strength—it can actually help them feel more stable.

Dealing with Disappointment

Disappointment can happen if a plan does not succeed or if someone breaks a promise. Capricorns feel it sharply because they invest effort and trust with care. They might react by becoming even more focused on making things right. If they cannot fix the disappointment, they could go through a period of sadness or confusion. Eventually, they try to learn from what went wrong and move forward. Yet, the emotional bruise can remain for a while, influencing how quickly they open up next time.

Comforting a Capricorn

If a Capricorn friend or family member seems upset but does not talk about it, a gentle approach can help. Asking, "Would you like to talk, or would you like me to just be here?" can show them they have options. Practical support—like offering to help with a task—can also demonstrate kindness. Most importantly, avoid pushing them to spill emotions right away. Respect their pace, and let them know you are there if and when they choose to share. Over time, this respectful approach can help a Capricorn feel safe enough to open up.

Trust and Emotional Sharing

Capricorns often need proof that someone is reliable before sharing deeper emotions. If the person has proven trustworthiness through consistent, respectful behavior, Capricorn may gradually reveal more. The bond that forms can be very strong because Capricorn does not take emotional sharing lightly. If betrayed, though, they might withdraw for a long time or never fully open up to that person again. Emotional trust is a serious matter to them, and once broken, it is hard to fix.

Capricorn's Sense of Duty and Emotions

A significant part of Capricorn's emotional life is tied to duty. They feel responsible for family, friends, work, and their own expectations. If they cannot meet these responsibilities, anxiety or guilt can arise. They might push themselves harder, skipping rest or ignoring personal needs. Over time, this can lead to burnout. Learning to set realistic limits and say "no" when necessary is crucial. This helps them protect their mental and emotional energy.

Pride in Small Achievements

While Capricorn can be very ambitious, they also find comfort in achieving everyday goals. Finishing tasks or helping a friend can bring them a calm sense of pride. This positive feeling is an emotional lift that reminds them their efforts matter. They might not brag about these achievements, but inside, they feel more confident and secure. These small wins can keep them emotionally steady, especially when bigger goals are far away.

Adapting to Change

Sudden changes can trigger emotional unease for Capricorn. They prefer a predictable environment. If a shift happens—like moving to a new place, changing schools, or losing a job—they might experience anxiety or sadness. They may take extra time to adjust, and they might seem distant or stressed during the process. However, once they accept the new reality, they create structure in the changed situation. This helps them regain emotional balance. Gradually, they discover they can handle change, even if it is uncomfortable at first.

Comparisons to Other Signs

People might compare Capricorn's emotional expression to signs that are more open or expressive, mistakenly thinking Capricorn lacks feelings. In truth, Capricorn simply handles emotions in a different way. They value steady progress, quiet reflection, and practical action over dramatic displays. If someone appreciates the Capricorn's style, they can enjoy a supportive connection that does not rely on constant emotional flare-ups.

Healthy vs. Unhealthy Emotional Patterns

A healthy Capricorn deals with worries by creating achievable plans and seeking help when needed. They allow themselves some relaxation or fun. An unhealthy pattern appears if they bury all emotions, never ask for support, or work until they are exhausted. They might become overly critical of themselves or lash out in cold ways. Recognizing these warning signs helps Capricorns change course. They can remind themselves that it is acceptable to rest and share concerns with people they trust.

Finding Emotional Confidence

Over time, many Capricorns learn that their emotional depth is a strength, not a weakness. By carefully examining their feelings, they gain insight into themselves. They can use these insights to build better relationships, set boundaries, and maintain personal well-being. Developing the courage to show a bit more emotion with trusted people can lead to stronger bonds. Step by step, they balance their natural caution with healthy openness.

Interactions with Highly Emotional People

When paired with someone who expresses strong emotions easily, Capricorn might initially feel overwhelmed. However, they can learn from each other. Capricorn can show how logic and steady methods help manage problems. Meanwhile, the other person can teach Capricorn that letting emotions out can be healing. Both sides need patience. Capricorn might say, "I want to understand your feelings," and the other person can make an effort to communicate them calmly. This exchange can enrich both parties' emotional skills.

Encouraging Self-Reflection

One way Capricorns deepen emotional awareness is by reflecting on their day before sleep or while taking a quiet walk. They might ask themselves, "What made me happy or upset today?" By naming these feelings, they start to see patterns. If something causes repeated stress, they can look for solutions. If something brings them happiness, they can include more of it in their schedule. This self-reflection helps them understand that emotions are signals, guiding them to improve their lives in small but important ways.

Conclusion

Behind Capricorn's calm appearance lies a rich emotional world. They often work carefully through each feeling, preferring logic and caution over public displays of emotion. While this can appear distant, it allows them to handle stress and responsibilities without becoming overwhelmed. As they grow, many Capricorns learn that showing vulnerability can be a source of true strength. By respecting their need for privacy while also welcoming trusted support, they find balance. In this way, their emotional depth becomes a stable foundation for personal growth, meaningful connections, and a satisfying sense of self.

CHAPTER 10: STRENGTHS THAT HELP CAPRICORN SUCCEED

Understanding Capricorn's Core Strengths

Each zodiac sign is said to come with certain advantages. For Capricorn, these strengths revolve around responsibility, patience, and a steady approach to challenges. They are often the ones who keep going, even when others give up. Rather than making big leaps, Capricorns prefer sure steps that lead to real progress. These strengths help them in many areas of life—from school to hobbies to the workplace.

Reliability and Dedication

One of Capricorn's greatest strengths is reliability. If they promise to do something, they typically follow through. This makes them a strong choice for tasks that require consistent effort over time. Whether it is completing a homework project or managing a complex assignment at work, they aim to deliver results. People around them often appreciate that they do not quit halfway. This dedication can build trust and respect in both personal and professional circles.

Patience and Steady Progress

Capricorns tend to prefer a steady climb rather than a quick rush. If they set a goal, they will work on it step by step, rarely expecting overnight success. This patience means they do not become frustrated as quickly as those who want instant results. They might face hurdles along the way, but their calm mindset keeps them focused. Over months or even years, they can see big achievements come to life because they did not give up after the first setback.

Practical Problem-Solving

Another strength is Capricorn's skill at solving problems in a real-world way. They are not afraid to roll up their sleeves and work through practical steps. If a friend needs help fixing something, Capricorn might look for a reliable manual or method. If a family member is stressed about finances, Capricorn can help create a budget. They prefer solid fixes over wild guesses, making them dependable when a serious issue arises. This ability to apply logic and structure is a huge asset in many life situations.

Clear Sense of Responsibility

Capricorn often feels a deep inner drive to fulfill duties. If a Capricorn is assigned a task, they see it as their responsibility to complete it as well as possible. This sense of duty can push them to learn new skills or stay up late if the project demands it. While this sometimes leads to stress, it can also result in achievements that earn admiration from teachers, bosses, or peers. Their sense of responsibility also extends to relationships. They try not to break promises or forget commitments to others.

Discipline and Self-Control

Discipline is a key trait for many Capricorns. They can set personal rules to keep themselves on track. For example, if they decide they want to exercise more, they might plan a schedule and stick to it, even when they do not feel like it. Similarly, if they aim to save money, they can cut back on small luxuries to meet their goal. This self-control can help them resist impulsive decisions that might harm them in the long run.

Ability to Organize and Plan

Being organized is a major strength. Capricorns can break down tasks into smaller parts and manage them without confusion. Whether it is planning an event, overseeing a school club, or coordinating a work project, they think about the needed resources and steps. This reduces chaos and boosts efficiency. Their planning mindset also helps them foresee challenges. For instance, they might gather extra supplies or create a backup plan just in case something goes wrong.

Focused Determination

Once a Capricorn sets a goal, they have strong focus. They generally do not get distracted by unimportant details. This determination can help them excel in activities like sports, music, or any pursuit that requires regular practice. They believe in incremental gains, trusting that small efforts add up over time. Even if progress is slow, they keep their eye on the prize. This unwavering stance often sets them apart from those who lose interest quickly.

Respect for Structure and Order

Capricorn's respect for order gives them an edge in situations where rules or guidelines exist. They do not mind following a structured system if it leads to stable outcomes. In a chaotic environment, they might be the one who brings a plan to calm things down. This respect for rules also makes them good at understanding how complex processes work, because they are willing to read instructions and follow steps without skipping anything.

Calm Under Pressure

Another strength is Capricorn's ability to remain calm when problems arise. Instead of panicking, they tend to search for a way to fix what is wrong. They think logically, asking what needs to be done first, second, and so on. This makes them very useful in emergencies. Others might look to Capricorn for guidance because they offer clear solutions rather than fear-based reactions. Their calm approach can keep a group focused on solutions instead of getting lost in anxiety.

Dependable Team Player

Although Capricorns can work well alone, they are also dependable in groups. They want a team to succeed and do their part without making excuses. If something needs to be done, they often volunteer if they have the skills. They do not seek applause; they prefer to quietly make progress. Teammates usually appreciate that Capricorn keeps the group on schedule and does not vanish in the middle of tasks. This reliability can lead to leadership roles, even if Capricorn did not initially aim for them.

Realistic Goal-Setting

Some people set goals that are too grand or unrealistic, but Capricorn usually sets targets they believe they can reach with effort. This realism prevents frequent disappointment. Instead, they pick a level that is challenging but not impossible. When they achieve one goal, they move on to a slightly bigger one. Over time, these step-by-step achievements can lead to major success without the emotional roller-coaster that comes from chasing unreachable aims.

Willingness to Learn

Capricorns often like to expand their knowledge or skills if it helps them handle duties more effectively. If they see a gap in what they know, they will quietly research, practice, or seek advice from an expert. This continuous growth helps them stay relevant in their chosen field or hobby. They do not rely on luck; they prefer to sharpen their abilities. This willingness to learn also means they can adapt when life throws them a challenge that requires a new approach.

Long-Term Thinking

While some people focus on short-term thrills, Capricorns look down the road. They consider how their current choices might affect the future. This can help them avoid reckless behaviors, such as spending all their savings on something temporary. They often prepare for potential problems by saving money or learning skills that might be needed later. This careful thinking can give them a sense of stability that others admire.

Staying Grounded

Capricorn is an earth sign, and this often shows up as being grounded in reality. They do not usually get carried away by unrealistic dreams. Instead, they check if a plan is workable before starting. This sense of realism can protect them from investing time or money into something that will not pay off. It also helps them handle disappointment because they understand that life involves some ups and downs, and stable effort will see them through.

Respect for Hard Effort

Capricorns generally believe that reliable results come from steady and honest effort. They are not easily tempted by shortcuts or quick fixes unless they have tested them and see they truly work. This respect for genuine work can guide them away from questionable schemes. It also means they appreciate when others put in real effort. They may be drawn to mentors or examples of people who achieved lasting success through practice and persistence.

Ability to Self-Motivate

Some people need external motivation, like rewards or constant praise, but Capricorn often finds motivation within. If they set a goal, they push themselves to do it, even if nobody else is watching. This self-sufficiency can bring satisfaction, knowing they do not rely on outside applause to keep going. They define their own milestones and celebrate them internally (using "celebrate" in the sense of quietly acknowledging a milestone, rather than a grand festivity). This makes them resilient during times when external support might be lacking.

Strong Moral Compass

Many Capricorns hold themselves to a high standard of honesty and fairness. They want to do what is right, even if it is not the easiest path. This moral sense helps them keep a good reputation. People trust them because they see that Capricorn is not likely to cheat or lie for personal gain. This trust can open doors in personal relationships and career opportunities. Others might seek Capricorn's opinion on difficult ethical choices, respecting their balanced viewpoint.

Practical Creativity

While some might think of Capricorn as not very creative, they can be inventive in down-to-earth ways. They may design a new method to handle daily tasks or come up with clever solutions for tight budgets. Their creativity is often guided by practicality, so they craft ideas that can actually work. This inventive streak, combined with logic, can lead to valuable results. They may not flaunt wild art pieces, but they demonstrate creativity in how they solve real-world problems.

Steadfast Loyalty

Capricorns can be highly loyal to people or causes that align with their values. If they feel a friend or colleague is worth supporting, they will stand by them through difficulties. This loyalty is steady rather than showy. They might check in with someone who is struggling, offer help, or speak up for them if needed. Over time, others see that Capricorn does not abandon people just because the situation is tough. This reliability builds meaningful, long-lasting bonds.

Foresight in Decision-Making

Because they anticipate potential pitfalls, Capricorns often weigh the pros and cons of decisions carefully. They do not like being caught off guard. This foresight means they might ask questions such as, "What if this goes wrong?" or "Do we have another plan if that happens?" Some might see this as cautious, but it actually prevents bigger failures. By thinking of backup plans, Capricorns avoid sudden disasters and keep moving forward.

Modest Confidence

Capricorns can be quietly confident in their abilities. They do not always boast about what they can do. Instead, they let their work speak for itself. This modest style can be refreshing in environments where many people try to outdo each other with big claims. Over time, others notice that Capricorn consistently delivers, gaining respect without loud self-praise. This combination of confidence and modesty can create a strong, stable presence that people trust.

Earning Respect Through Consistency

A powerful advantage Capricorn holds is their knack for showing the same level of effort and honesty over time. This consistency can be more impressive than a single flashy success. It shows that they do not rely on luck or fleeting energy bursts, but on steady, reliable actions. Over years, this can earn them a reputation as someone who can be counted on in almost any situation, which might bring them leadership roles or special responsibilities.

Realistic Self-Assessment

Capricorns often know their own strengths and limits quite well. They might say, "I am good at organizing, but not so strong at public speaking," for example. This honesty with themselves helps them pick tasks that match their skill set or plan for improvements in areas where they are weaker. It also shields them from biting off more than they can handle. Knowing themselves leads to better, more thoughtful decisions about how to spend time and energy.

Emphasis on Quality

In many parts of life, Capricorn looks for and produces quality. They prefer to own a few well-made items rather than many cheap ones. When working on a project, they aim for a solid result rather than a hasty job. This emphasis on quality can set them apart in a world where speed often matters more. People notice that Capricorn's work or suggestions tend to hold up over time, reflecting careful thought and high standards.

Overcoming Obstacles with Persistence

Life has a way of throwing unexpected barriers. Capricorn's typical response is to observe the obstacle, form a realistic plan, and keep pushing until it is overcome. If one method fails, they try another. They might appear stubborn at times, but in a positive sense—they do not easily back down from a challenge they believe they can solve. This stick-with-it mindset often leads to breakthroughs that others miss because they gave up too soon.

Teaching by Example

Capricorns might not give long speeches about success or how to reach goals, but they often teach others simply by doing. Younger siblings, friends, or coworkers might see how Capricorn handles a tough task and learn from it. Capricorn's calm, steady approach can inspire others to adopt similar methods. Even without formal teaching, their behavior and outcomes show people the power of slow, consistent effort paired with realistic aims.

Putting All Strengths Together

When we look at these strengths as a whole—reliability, patience, discipline, practical thinking, loyalty, and more—we can see why Capricorns so often manage to reach important goals. They do not rely on luck or sudden bursts of enthusiasm. Instead, they build step by step, trust their ability to handle challenges, and persist when the path is tough. By knowing these strengths, Capricorns can play to them in everyday life. They can choose paths that let their skills shine, or use their natural style to improve any situation.

Conclusion

Capricorns have many qualities that lead to lasting results. They are loyal, patient, organized, and committed to doing their best. They trust in hard effort and value honesty. They might not shout about their abilities, but they show them through consistent, focused work. In relationships and work settings, their steady approach often brings stability and a sense of reassurance to those around them. By embracing these strengths, Capricorns can tackle challenges, grow in confidence, and lay the groundwork for solid achievements throughout their lives.

CHAPTER 11: WEAKNESSES AND CHALLENGES FOR CAPRICORN

Why Look at Weaknesses?

Just as each zodiac sign may have strengths, there are also drawbacks or hurdles that can appear. Recognizing weaknesses is a useful step, because it helps people figure out areas that need extra attention. Capricorns are often seen as capable and calm, but they are still human. They can stumble in certain ways, and they might have habits that make their lives more stressful. By identifying these points, Capricorns can try to address them and avoid bigger troubles.

Being Too Hard on Themselves

One major issue for Capricorns is that they set very high standards for what they want to achieve. At times, these standards can become so high that they feel impossible to reach. This can lead to a lot of pressure on the Capricorn. If something goes wrong or results take longer than expected, they might blame themselves too harshly. That critical voice in their mind might say, "I should have done better." Over time, this self-criticism can affect confidence and happiness.

Fear of Taking Risks

Because Capricorns prefer a steady path, they may turn away from risks that could lead to growth or interesting chances. They might stick with comfortable plans rather than trying new ideas. In many situations, being careful is good. However, if a Capricorn always avoids anything unfamiliar, they can miss out on new possibilities.

This fear of the unknown can make them feel stuck if they never consider a different path.

Work-Life Imbalance

Capricorns are known for their dedication. They can spend long hours trying to perfect a task or solve a problem. Yet, this focus on work or responsibilities can become all-consuming. Some Capricorns find it hard to relax because they always think there is more to do. They might check messages at night, skip social events, or postpone rest. This imbalance can lead to tiredness or feeling distant from loved ones. Over time, they might lose the energy that once made them effective.

Stubbornness and Resistance to Change

A Capricorn's reliable approach sometimes becomes stubbornness. If they have decided on a method, they can be slow to adapt when the situation shifts. They might insist that their way is correct, even if there are valid reasons to modify it. If a friend or coworker suggests a new approach, they might doubt it. This resistance to change can stop them from discovering better solutions. It can also cause friction with others who want to try something different.

Struggle with Showing Feelings

Capricorns can have a tough time expressing deeper emotions. People in their lives might think they are distant or uncaring. In reality, Capricorns might feel a great deal but find it hard to say it out loud. This can block true closeness in relationships. If they fail to share warmth or vulnerability, their loved ones might not sense a strong bond. They risk seeming cold when they simply need time and comfort to open up.

Overthinking and Worry

A Capricorn might overanalyze decisions or events, fearing all the "what ifs." Their logical mind can be a gift, but it can also turn into a source of stress if they cannot quiet their thoughts. This habit of imagining worst-case outcomes could keep them awake at night. While caution can help avoid mistakes, endless worrying uses mental energy. It prevents them from enjoying the present moment and can lead to second-guessing many daily choices.

Difficulty Delegating Tasks

Capricorns can be so determined to ensure everything is done well that they rarely trust others to help. They might think, "I know how to do this right; I should do it myself." As a result, they end up with too many tasks. This can lead to burnout, and it also keeps them from building teamwork skills. In a group or family setting, other people can feel left out if Capricorn never allows them to contribute. Learning to share tasks can ease the pressure and improve collaboration.

Rigid Planning

Planning is a strong suit for Capricorns, but it becomes a weakness if they are not flexible when unexpected things happen. Life rarely follows a perfect plan. If a schedule changes or a project takes a new direction, Capricorn might feel frustrated or unsettled. They might keep trying to push the original plan, even though the situation no longer fits. This lack of flexibility can cause stress and missed chances for simpler or better paths.

Tendency to Compare Themselves

Capricorns set goals and measure progress. However, they might also compare themselves to others who seem more successful. This comparison can lead them to feel that they are never doing enough, even when they are making steady progress. Focusing on what other people have or do can overshadow their own wins. This habit can create a negative loop of self-doubt, rather than encouraging healthy motivation.

Reluctance to Ask for Help

Capricorns can believe they should handle challenges on their own. They might see asking for help as a sign of weakness or an inconvenience to others. Because of this mindset, they might struggle alone, even when people around them are ready to assist. Over time, this can escalate stress, making tasks harder than they need to be. Allowing others to help can actually strengthen bonds and reveal easier ways of solving problems.

Risk of Becoming Isolated

Because Capricorns often keep a calm, focused front, they might not appear as if they want company or support. Others may assume Capricorn is fine alone. Over time, Capricorn could feel lonely without clear connections. They might not reach out to friends or loved ones, assuming that everything is under control. This isolation can lead to a sense of emptiness. Even though they might not express it, Capricorns benefit from social interaction and emotional closeness like anyone else.

Harsh Judgment of Others

A Capricorn might hold others to the same high standards they set for themselves. This can result in seeing people as careless or lazy if they do not share the same level of discipline. However, not everyone manages tasks the same way. Quick judgment can strain friendships or work relationships, especially if Capricorn does not recognize the variety of styles and abilities among people. Showing understanding can lead to healthier bonds and better teamwork.

Perfectionism

The combination of high standards, fear of mistakes, and caution about others' work can lead to perfectionism. While aiming for quality is admirable, perfectionism can trap Capricorns in endless tweaks or a fear of finishing. They might waste time making minor improvements or hold back projects because they do not think it is "good enough." Learning to accept that something can be good without being flawless is an important step in letting go of this burden.

Dependence on External Approval

Even though Capricorns often prefer to work quietly, they may secretly crave validation that they are on the right path. If no one acknowledges their efforts, they might question themselves. Over time, they can become too reliant on praise from certain sources, like a boss or a parent. If that praise disappears, they might feel lost. Building self-approval is essential, so they do not tie their self-worth entirely to outside opinions.

Guarding Personal Problems

When Capricorns face personal troubles—maybe with finances, relationships, or health—they might hide these issues instead of seeking help. They could think they must keep up a strong front, or they worry people will judge them if they admit a struggle. Unfortunately, bottling up serious matters can lead to bigger crises. Sharing problems with trusted individuals can help Capricorns see solutions more clearly and reduce the pressure they feel.

Strong Reaction to Failure

Failure or rejection can hurt a Capricorn deeply. They might view it as evidence that they fell short of their responsibilities. While some people shake off failure as part of learning, Capricorns might dwell on it for a long time, feeling they have disappointed themselves or others. This can lead to low spirits and hesitation to try again. Recognizing that failure is often just an event—not a permanent flaw—can help them recover faster.

Unwillingness to Let Go of Control

Some Capricorns want to be in charge because they trust their own careful approach. They can struggle to relax in settings where they must rely on another person's decisions. For instance, if they are on a team where someone else is the leader, they may feel uneasy or attempt to steer the process from behind the scenes. Learning to trust others' leadership and methods can ease tension and open the door to new perspectives.

Emotional Bottlenecks

By rarely discussing what is on their mind, Capricorns can build up worries or sadness until it becomes too large to handle calmly. This can cause them to snap at seemingly small irritations. Loved ones might be caught off guard by these sudden mood swings, since Capricorn usually appears steady. Finding a more frequent outlet—such as talking to a friend or writing in a journal—can prevent these emotional bottlenecks from happening.

Overemphasis on Material Security

A desire for a stable life can turn into an overemphasis on money or status if Capricorn is not mindful. They could lose sight of other joys in the quest to feel financially or socially secure. They might take a job they do not enjoy just for a higher salary, or push themselves to earn prestige in a way that compromises their well-being. Balancing practical needs with personal happiness can prevent this pitfall.

Difficulty Relaxing and Having Fun

Although many Capricorns do know how to enjoy themselves, some struggle to let loose. They might feel guilty if they are not always being productive, or they may see leisure time as wasted. This can limit their ability to recharge. A lack of fun can also make life dull, fueling stress rather than releasing it. Recognizing that breaks and hobbies are important for mental health can help Capricorns maintain energy over the long term.

Unexpressed Ambitions

A Capricorn might have big ambitions, yet keep them hidden. They might fear that telling people about these aims could lead to embarrassment if the goals are not reached. While caution is natural, never sharing or pursuing these hopes can turn into regret. Speaking about a goal with trusted allies can lead to feedback or opportunities that push Capricorn forward. Sometimes, the biggest challenge is taking that first step of revealing what they truly want.

Neglect of Emotional Bonds

Because Capricorns can be career-focused or duties-focused, they might forget to make time for deep, personal connections. They might miss important moments with family or skip calls with friends, always thinking they will catch up later. Over time, these relationships could fade. This can lead to sadness or regret if they wake up one day realizing they did not nurture their closest bonds. Making room for shared experiences can prevent these ties from weakening.

Resenting Dependence

Capricorns typically value self-sufficiency. If they find themselves in a situation where they must rely on someone—like a partner during an illness or a coworker who has a needed skill—they can feel uneasy. They might resent the fact that they cannot handle everything alone. This attitude can strain relationships. It is important for Capricorns to realize that healthy interdependence does not mean they are weak. Relying on each other is normal and can bring people closer.

Being Overly Cautious in Relationships

In romantic or close friendships, Capricorns can come across as hesitating to commit too soon. They might hold back on saying how they feel, waiting until they are 100% sure. This can cause the other person to assume Capricorn lacks affection. Over time, the bond might remain stuck at a shallow level because of Capricorn's fear of vulnerability. Finding a healthy middle ground can help them form strong, lasting connections without feeling rushed.

Taking Criticism Personally

Constructive criticism is meant to help people grow, but Capricorns might take it as a sign of personal failure. Rather than using the feedback to improve, they could feel wounded or brood over the words. This can damage their willingness to cooperate or try new methods. If Capricorns learn to separate the idea that critique is an attack on them as a person, they can gain insights and become even better at what they do.

Unrealistic Self-Expectations

Some Capricorns set extreme targets: perfect success at work, flawless relationships, ideal finances, and more. While aiming high can be motivating, trying to handle all these areas at a top level all at once is hard. They might burn out if they do not let themselves be human. The real challenge is picking what matters most, focusing on that, and giving themselves grace in other areas. Perfection is rarely possible, and chasing it can lead to exhaustion.

Turning Weaknesses into Growth

Recognizing these weaknesses is not about being negative. Instead, it is a chance for Capricorns to reflect on what might be getting in their way. Each problem or habit can be managed with mindful steps. For instance, if fear of failure is holding them back, they can set smaller objectives so they feel safer about taking action. If they have trouble showing feelings, they can practice sharing small emotions with someone they trust. Bit by bit, these efforts can lift the burdens that weaknesses create.

CHAPTER 12: CAPRICORN AND PHYSICAL WELL-BEING

Why Physical Well-Being Matters

A Capricorn's drive for stability and success can extend to health as well. Although they may focus on work or goals, they also gain from having a healthy body. When Capricorns feel strong physically, they can better handle daily tasks, think more clearly, and maintain steady emotions. Physical well-being is not just about looking a certain way; it is about having energy, endurance, and confidence to tackle each day without feeling worn down.

General Attitude Toward Health

Capricorns tend to value practical approaches. If they see a clear routine or method that improves health, they are often willing to try it. They like step-by-step plans and may adopt health goals such as setting aside a certain time for exercise or preparing meals. However, they sometimes put these plans aside if work or other responsibilities feel more pressing. Balancing their natural sense of duty with self-care is vital, so they do not run themselves ragged.

Structured Approach to Fitness

Just as Capricorns enjoy structure in other parts of life, they often do well with a steady fitness plan. This might be going to the gym on set days of the week, following a guided exercise program, or practicing a sport that has clear rules. They like seeing progress over time. Keeping a simple chart or tracking app can help them note improvements, which in turn boosts their motivation. They typically do not need flashy workouts; a consistent routine suits them.

Preferring Safe, Reliable Exercises

While some signs might love high-adrenaline activities, Capricorns tend to pick exercises that feel reliable and less risky. They could gravitate toward walking, jogging, swimming, yoga, or weight training with proper form. They want to avoid injuries that might hinder their ability to handle work or home tasks. Of course, there are exceptions—some Capricorns might enjoy adventurous sports. But in general, they like forms of exercise where they can plan, track, and see progress clearly.

Diet and Nutrition

In terms of eating habits, Capricorns might enjoy meals that provide real nutritional benefits. They may research certain vitamins or minerals to ensure they stay healthy. However, they can also slip into convenience foods if they are swamped with work. A good system for meal planning can help them stay on track. They might plan a weekly menu, use grocery lists, and cook batches of food at once to save time. This organized style suits Capricorn's preference for efficiency.

Practical Meal Planning

Because Capricorns often like stability, they might be okay with repeating certain healthy meals. For example, they might have a favorite balanced breakfast they eat most days. This consistency saves time and mental energy. Some Capricorns also enjoy learning about simple cooking methods. They might try basic recipes that give them healthy carbs, proteins, and fats. By removing guesswork, they reduce the risk of grabbing less nutritious snacks on the go.

Challenges in Maintaining Physical Health

Work overload is a major obstacle. Capricorns can get so caught up in tasks that they skip meals or forget to drink enough water. They might sacrifice sleep to finish a project, telling themselves they will rest later. Over time, these small neglects add up, weakening the body's resilience. Another challenge is that Capricorns can be tough on themselves, expecting perfect results in their health plan. If they fail to meet a goal, they might feel discouraged or give up, even though gradual progress is what truly matters.

Stress and Its Physical Effects

A Capricorn's mind can hold onto worries, whether they are about job performance, finances, or personal goals. Stress affects the body by increasing tension, which can lead to headaches, trouble sleeping, or other issues. If Capricorns do not address stress properly, they may end up feeling constantly tired. Finding ways to manage stress—such as moderate exercise, breaks during the day, or relaxation methods—can help them stay physically strong and reduce burnout.

Importance of Regular Checkups

Because Capricorns like to feel in control, they might ignore symptoms, hoping they will vanish. They could see going to the doctor as admitting a weakness or losing productive time. In reality, regular checkups and early care can prevent bigger problems. A systematic approach to health includes setting routine visits with healthcare professionals. This way, they can catch issues early and make changes before small concerns turn into major ones.

Sleep Habits

Good sleep is crucial for everyone, and Capricorns might especially need it because they tend to use their brains a lot for planning and problem-solving. Yet they can have trouble switching off at night. They might lie awake, thinking about tasks. Creating a regular bedtime can help. They might lower lights an hour before bed, stop checking messages, and do a calming activity like reading. This signals their mind to settle. If they set a specific wake-up time, it can help stabilize their internal clock.

Finding Motivations for Health

Capricorns generally do well when they have a tangible goal. For health, it might be having more energy, being able to climb stairs without getting winded, or reducing stress so they can think clearly. By breaking health targets into smaller steps—for example, losing a modest amount of weight over a realistic timeframe or improving stamina by exercising three times a week—they stay motivated. They also like tracking progress through numbers or charts, seeing how each small step adds up.

Physical Activities That Suit Capricorn

- **Walking or Hiking:** Simple, reliable, and can fit into a daily routine.

- **Yoga or Pilates:** Builds core strength and flexibility in a measured way.

- **Swimming:** Offers a full-body workout with little strain on the joints.

- **Steady Cardio (Cycling, Elliptical):** Allows them to monitor pace and duration.

- **Weight Training:** Encourages slow but steady gains in strength, which appeals to their methodical mindset.

They do not have to do all of these; picking one or two that fit their schedule and interests is a good start.

Avoiding Extreme Diets or Methods

Capricorns usually prefer balanced solutions over extreme trends. If a diet seems too drastic or a fitness routine appears too risky, they might stay away. Still, some might be tempted by quick fixes if they feel pressured. This can be risky. Extreme diets may lead to short-term outcomes but cause health problems down the road. Choosing moderate approaches that can be sustained is better for Capricorn's long-term well-being.

Sticking to Routines

Once they develop a routine, Capricorns are often consistent about following it. This is a big advantage for building healthy habits. However, if their routine is disrupted—such as travel, illness, or a busy period at work—they might find it hard to jump back in. Recognizing that life will have interruptions can help them plan for alternatives. For example, if they cannot reach the gym, maybe they can do a short workout at home or go for a walk during lunch.

Caring for the Skeletal System

Some traditions associate Capricorn with joints and bones, partly because Capricorn is an earth sign linked to structure. Whether or not someone believes in that, paying attention to bone health is wise. Eating foods rich in calcium, getting enough vitamin D (through sunlight or supplements), and doing weight-bearing exercise all support strong bones. Since Capricorns often like planning, they can schedule a few workouts each week that challenge their bones gently—like brisk walking or weight exercises.

Mind-Body Approaches

Because stress can build up, Capricorns can benefit from activities that nurture mental calmness while helping the body. Techniques like meditation, gentle stretching, or slower-paced exercises can relax tense muscles and calm the mind. They might resist these at first if they see them as unproductive or too slow. However, once they notice reduced stress and better focus, they might find them valuable parts of a healthy routine.

Balancing Physical and Mental Well-Being

Physical health and mental health are linked. If Capricorn's mind is anxious or overwhelmed, it can lead to neglect of the body. Conversely, if the body is tired or undernourished, it can feed more worry. Finding a harmony between physical activities, adequate rest, and mental relaxation is key. This includes scheduling down-time, saying "no" to extra commitments when already busy, and recognizing signals of mental fatigue before they become severe.

Healthy Competitiveness

In some cases, Capricorns might feel motivated by mild competition. For example, they could join a friend in tracking daily steps or team up with a coworker for a fitness challenge. However, they should watch out for pushing themselves too hard for the sake of winning. A friendly rivalry can be fun, but not if it leads to injury or stress. The main focus should remain on steady improvement rather than immediate victory.

Common Pitfalls

- **Skipping Meals:** Busy Capricorns might skip meals to save time, leading to low energy and possible overeating later.

- **Ignoring Warning Signs:** They may dismiss aches, pains, or fatigue, which can become bigger problems.

- **Overconsumption of Caffeine:** Some Capricorns lean on coffee or tea to push through tasks, which can cause jitters or disrupt sleep if overdone.

- **Sedentary Habits:** If they sit at a desk too long without breaks, stiffness or poor posture can arise.

By spotting these tendencies, Capricorns can make small changes to avoid them.

Healthy Ways to Release Energy

Capricorns often carry tension from their day. Physical activities like going for a brisk walk, doing a quick set of stretches, or even tidying up a room can help them let go of that tension. They can also explore hobbies that involve gentle movement—like gardening, dancing in a low-pressure environment, or slow martial arts (such as Tai Chi). Releasing energy in these ways keeps stress from building to an unhealthy level.

Setting Realistic Goals

A Capricorn might say, "I will work out five days a week, two hours each time," without considering the rest of their schedule. That can lead to disappointment if they cannot keep it up. A better plan is starting with smaller goals. For instance, a 30-minute workout three times a week can be more doable. Once they see success, they can adjust the routine in a way that aligns with their lifestyle.

Hydration and Simple Wellness

Being practical, Capricorns might appreciate direct, easy tips, like drinking enough water. They can keep a reusable water bottle and aim to empty it a certain number of times a day. Similarly, taking short breaks to stand up and stretch if they work at a desk can do wonders for circulation and posture. These small, consistent acts can have a big impact on overall health without feeling time-consuming.

Social Support for Fitness

Though Capricorns can be private, having a workout buddy or a friend who shares health interests can keep them on track. They might hesitate to rely on someone else, but light accountability can be helpful. If they know someone is waiting for them at the gym, they are less likely to skip. Even occasional check-ins with a friend about progress can reinforce healthy habits.

Body Awareness

Some Capricorns focus so much on external tasks that they do not pay attention to signals from their own bodies—like hunger, thirst, or tiredness. Over time, ignoring these signs can lead to bigger health problems. Practicing body awareness means pausing occasionally to check in: "Am I hungry? Do I need a glass of water? Are my shoulders tense?" Then they can address the need before it becomes a bigger concern.

Mindful Relaxation

After a demanding day, a Capricorn might feel that simply lying on the couch is the best form of rest. While this can help physically, adding a mindfulness element—like gentle breathing exercises or calming music—can deepen the relaxation. A short walk in a peaceful place or a quiet hobby like coloring can help settle the mind. This mindful rest can lower stress hormones, supporting better sleep and overall recovery.

Rewarding Oneself in Healthy Ways

If Capricorns meet certain health goals, they might want to reward themselves. Rather than using rewards that could hurt their progress (like overindulging in unhealthy snacks), they might choose practical treats. For example, a new pair of running shoes or a comfortable yoga mat could keep them motivated. They might also enjoy scheduling a massage or a relaxing spa visit. Such positive rewards encourage them to maintain good habits.

Staying Motivated When Results Are Slow

Capricorns are used to gradual improvements, but it can still be discouraging if a scale number or endurance level does not change as fast as hoped. Remembering that real progress often takes weeks or months can help them stay patient. They might keep a simple diary of how they feel after workouts or how their energy levels improve. This broader perspective can be more useful than just looking at numbers that might fluctuate day to day.

Conclusion

For Capricorns, physical well-being fits naturally with their love for consistency and organization. By creating realistic exercise schedules, planning balanced meals, and keeping track of their progress, they can steadily improve their health. It is also vital for them to notice the signals their bodies send, manage stress, and avoid overcommitting at work. When Capricorns find a balance between tasks and self-care, they are more likely to remain strong and focused for the long term. In this way, their steady nature and careful planning can lead to a secure, healthy lifestyle that supports all their other aims.

CHAPTER 13: CAPRICORN AND FINANCIAL MATTERS

Capricorn's Natural Caution Around Money

Many Capricorns are known for being thoughtful with their finances. They often prefer safety to risk, aiming to keep their money secure rather than diving into uncertain ventures. Some might consider them overly careful, but from a Capricorn's view, it is better to avoid sudden losses. This caution can be a helpful trait when the world around them changes quickly and people need solid planning. It also allows them to set aside savings little by little, which can add up over the years.

Early Lessons About Saving

In childhood or adolescence, Capricorns might notice how adults around them handle money. If they see poor spending habits, they could decide to do the opposite. If they see wise methods, they may follow that example. Even at a young age, a Capricorn can develop a habit of setting aside a portion of their allowance or earnings. By the time they reach adulthood, they may have learned to plan monthly budgets or keep track of spending. This steady approach helps them avoid financial chaos later on.

Practical Budgeting Skills

Capricorns typically enjoy order, so making a budget suits them. They might list all sources of income, then list their bills and essential expenses. After that, they see how much remains for saving or small comforts. Some use apps or spreadsheets to keep track, while others prefer a simple notebook. By reviewing this budget often, they can spot areas where they spend more than intended. They might also set financial goals, such as paying off a debt or saving for a large purchase. Their patience helps them reach these goals steadily.

Respect for Earning Through Effort

Because they value real work, Capricorns often believe money should be earned through effort. They might be wary of fast schemes that promise huge rewards with little work. They know that if something sounds too good to be true, it likely is. This mindset can protect them from fraud or risky gambles. It also encourages them to focus on stable income sources, whether that is a steady job, freelancing, or running a small business with firm fundamentals.

Tendency to Plan for the Long Term

Capricorns typically do not make decisions based only on the next few days or weeks. They look ahead, considering how a financial choice will shape their future. For instance, if they think about renting a home vs. buying one, they will weigh the pros and cons over many years. They might research the housing market or calculate how monthly payments compare to rent. This patient approach can help them avoid feeling rushed. It may also guide them to create safety nets like an emergency fund for unexpected costs.

Goal-Oriented Saving

Instead of saving blindly, Capricorns often like to set a clear purpose. For example, they might aim to save a certain amount for education, a down payment on a house, or a fund to start a small venture. This target gives them motivation, because they can see exactly how each saved dollar brings them closer to something important. They might track this progress on a chart or an app, feeling quietly proud as they get closer to their aim.

Responsible Use of Credit

Credit cards and loans are common in modern life, but Capricorns may be cautious about using them. They know credit can be helpful if managed well, but it can also lead to huge debt if used carelessly. If they do open a credit card, they prefer to pay it off in full each month rather than carry a balance. If they must take a loan—for a car or a house—they try to pick a payment plan they can truly afford. This thoughtful style helps them avoid being trapped by interest or fees.

Seeking Advice from Professionals

While Capricorns usually like to do their own research, they also see the value of expert guidance for complicated money matters. If they want to invest in markets or plan for retirement, they might talk to a trusted financial advisor. This does not mean they blindly accept all advice. They will likely ask thorough questions and compare suggestions with their own knowledge. But once they find an advisor they respect, they can form a lasting partnership that helps them create a solid financial roadmap.

Sticking to Sensible Investments

Capricorns are not typically eager to jump into wild investments. They look for stable options: dependable stocks, real estate, or funds with a steady track record. If they have some extra money to try more adventurous ventures, they do so with caution, only risking what they can afford to lose. They would rather see slow, consistent growth than gamble on something that might collapse overnight. While this approach might miss certain quick gains, it also avoids large-scale financial losses.

Handling Financial Stress

Even the best planners can face money problems—like sudden job loss or an unexpected medical bill. In such times, Capricorns often tap into their calm side. They might create a list of necessary expenses, cut out optional spending, and possibly pick up side work. Their mindset is to fix the problem step by step, rather than panic. However, financial stress can still weigh heavily on them, especially if they feel they failed. They might blame themselves, forgetting that some events are beyond anyone's control. Leaning on supportive friends or family can help them see they do not have to solve every crisis alone.

Generosity vs. Protectiveness

Because they work hard for their money, Capricorns can be protective of it. At times, people might see them as frugal or hesitant to lend money. However, Capricorns can be generous if they see the cause as worthy and safe. They might donate to an organization that aligns with their values or quietly help a family member with financial trouble. Yet they usually want proof that the money will be used responsibly. They do not enjoy seeing funds wasted.

Creating a Healthy Balance Between Saving and Spending

Some Capricorns become so focused on saving that they never allow themselves any treats. Others find a good balance, setting aside money for fun or relaxation, too. They might have a "fun fund" that holds a smaller part of their income, so they can purchase things they like without feeling guilty. If they do not set such limits, they might end up feeling deprived or resentful, which can lead to sudden splurges. Balance ensures they do not burn out from being overly strict.

Careful About Status Symbols

Capricorns may appreciate quality, like a sturdy car or well-made clothes, but they generally do not chase flashy items just to impress others. They prefer purchases that bring real value. However, in some situations, a Capricorn might see a nice home or car as a symbol of success they worked for. If that is the case, they will still think about long-term costs and maintenance before finalizing. They want to be sure they are not just spending to show off, but truly gaining something lasting in return.

Navigating Pay Negotiations

When negotiating pay or benefits at work, Capricorns can be cautious. They might not brag about their skills, so they risk being underpaid if they do not speak up. Learning how to ask confidently for what they are worth can be a challenge. They might gather data about average salaries, list their achievements, and calmly present a case for higher pay. Because they tend to be respectful and logical, many employers will see their points as fair. Over time, practicing negotiation skills can help them earn the income they truly deserve.

Handling Family Finances

Within a family, a Capricorn might be in charge of budgeting or paying bills. They like to keep track of due dates and confirm that everything is paid on time. If a family member has a carefree approach to money, Capricorn might feel stressed trying to maintain order. In such cases, it helps to have open chats about saving goals, expenses, and shared plans. By showing the benefits of a well-managed budget—like the ability to plan holidays or big purchases—Capricorn can guide others toward more balanced habits.

Teaching Children About Money

If a Capricorn has children or younger relatives, they often wish to pass on sound money lessons. They might give an allowance with rules about saving a part of it or encourage a teenager to get a part-time job to learn the value of effort. They may teach them to write down small financial goals, like buying a game or saving for a bigger item. This practical guidance can shape responsible habits, so young ones grow up confident in managing their own funds.

Overthinking Financial Decisions

On the flip side, Capricorns can get stuck analyzing multiple scenarios without making a move. They might worry they will pick the wrong investment or buy the wrong property. This fear of error can lead to missed chances. At some point, they might realize that no plan is completely risk-free, and the best route is to choose the option with the best balance of risk and reward. Accepting that they cannot predict the future can help them move forward instead of staying frozen by doubt.

Emergency Funds and Preparedness

A common piece of advice is to have an emergency fund covering a few months of living costs. This can give Capricorns a sense of safety, knowing they can handle a job loss or unexpected expense. If they reach that target, they might feel a quiet relief. This buffer can stop them from borrowing money at high interest or selling things in a rush. Because of their cautious style, Capricorns often see the value in preparing for what might go wrong before it ever does.

Avoiding Over-Control

Sometimes, a Capricorn might try to manage every single purchase in the household. This can strain relationships if others feel they have no say. Learning to trust a partner or family member with certain parts of the budget fosters cooperation. A Capricorn can still keep an overview, but they should allow loved ones some freedom. Otherwise, finances can become a source of arguments or resentment. A shared plan with space for personal spending works better than a strict set of do's and don'ts.

Financial Independence

Capricorns often value being in charge of their own finances. They might strive to be debt-free, have their own income, and not rely on others. This can be empowering. It can also, however, limit them if they refuse any form of collaboration. Sometimes, pooling resources with a trusted person can increase growth. For example, combining incomes to buy a property might be more feasible than doing it alone. The key is choosing partners carefully to avoid clashes in money style.

Staying Informed About Economic Changes

The world's economy shifts over time. Capricorns, who prefer stable ground, can benefit from reading about these changes. For instance, interest rates can rise or fall, or new financial tools may appear. By staying updated, they can adjust their plans sensibly. This does not require them to chase every new trend. Instead, they can watch what reliable sources say and decide whether changes might help or hinder their particular plans.

Balance Between Planning and Living

Some Capricorns save so much or focus so strongly on building a secure future that they forget to enjoy life's smaller delights. There is nothing wrong with wanting stability, but a life with zero pleasant treats can feel dull. Occasionally eating out with friends, watching a show, or taking a modest trip can bring happiness without wrecking the budget. By allocating a set portion for leisure, Capricorns can keep that sense of order yet also find moments of enjoyment in daily life.

Encouraging Others to Be Responsible

When they see friends or relatives being reckless with money, Capricorns might speak up. They might show them how to track expenses or suggest ways to cut useless costs. However, not everyone welcomes unsolicited advice, and it can create friction. A wiser approach is to offer help if asked, or to gently bring up money topics in a neutral way. If the other person shows interest, Capricorn can then share tips or resources. The aim is to guide, not to lecture.

Dealing with Financial Setbacks

Sometimes, despite careful planning, large setbacks happen. Maybe an investment goes bad, or they face unexpected job changes. While this can be upsetting, Capricorns usually do not stay defeated for long. They assess the damage, figure out how it happened, then piece together a fresh plan. They may reduce spending, find a temporary job, or sell unneeded items. This step-by-step method can be comforting during chaotic times, reminding them that they still have control over their future.

Healthy Mindset About Wealth

For Capricorns, wealth is often a way to feel safe. They do not necessarily crave huge riches just to show off. What they want is the freedom that comes from knowing they can handle problems without relying on others. While seeking this security, it is important that they do not let money become their only source of worth. Having good relationships, hobbies, and personal growth matters too. Money is a tool, not the only measure of a person's success or character.

Capricorn's Calm Influence on Friends' Finances

Friends sometimes look up to Capricorn's financial steadiness. They might see how a Capricorn avoids rash spending or keeps a clear budget. This can be an example for others who struggle with impulse buys or living paycheck to paycheck. If asked, Capricorns can share their methods, like keeping a simple expense log or dividing income into different categories. By remaining calm and practical, they inspire people who want to leave chaotic money habits behind.

Remaining Open to New Opportunities

While being careful is good, Capricorns should stay aware that new technology or markets can be profitable if approached wisely. They could explore fresh avenues—perhaps selling items online, or investing in a growing sector—if they see genuine promise. They should still do research and avoid rushing, but not dismiss new ideas just because they are unfamiliar. Striking a balance between caution and openness can lead to solid financial progress without big risks.

CHAPTER 14: HABITS AND SELF-REFLECTION FOR CAPRICORN

Why Habits Matter for Capricorn

Capricorns thrive on consistency. They like knowing what to expect from day to day, so habits can shape their life in a big way. Good habits, like regular exercise or organized planning, provide structure and help them meet their goals. Less helpful habits, such as overworking or being too rigid, can hold them back. Recognizing which habits truly serve them is key. Equally important is learning how to shift away from harmful patterns toward better ones.

Building Daily Routines

Many Capricorns enjoy having a set plan for each day. They might wake up at the same time, follow a morning process (like making the bed, preparing breakfast, and reading the news), then move through tasks in a specific order. This routine can bring a feeling of calm. They always know what comes next. It also saves mental energy, because they do not have to wonder when to eat, work, or rest. Over time, these small daily actions can build up to significant benefits, as each step supports progress.

Time Management as a Habit

One of Capricorn's strong points is managing time well. They might write down appointments, keep a calendar, or use phone reminders. By treating time as a valuable resource, they avoid rushing. They also reduce the risk of missing deadlines or forgetting responsibilities. That said, they can become too strict with scheduling if they do not allow for last-minute changes. Striking a balance—where a plan exists but can adapt if needed—is often the healthiest approach.

Setting Mini-Goals

Breaking large objectives into smaller steps suits Capricorn's steady style. They might have a long-term aim, like learning a skill or improving their overall well-being, but they realize it will not happen right away. So they form mini-goals, such as practicing for 30 minutes each day or finishing a certain part of a task each week. This process keeps them motivated, because they see measurable improvements. It also prevents them from feeling overwhelmed by the size of the main goal.

Avoiding Perfection in Routine

While building habits, Capricorns might chase the idea of a "perfect schedule." They may try to pack every hour with tasks and see any deviation as failure. This can lead to stress. No plan can be perfect all the time. Surprises happen, energy levels shift, and outside demands pop up. Learning to view a routine as a helpful guide—rather than an unbreakable law—makes it easier for Capricorns to adapt without feeling like they have messed everything up.

Reflecting on Progress

Self-reflection allows Capricorns to see if their habits are working. They might set aside time each week or month to look over what they have achieved and where they stumbled. For instance, if they aimed to go for a 20-minute walk every day, they can note how many times they actually did it. If they see they only walked three days out of seven, they can ask why. Was the goal unrealistic, or did something else come up? This gentle review helps them improve habits rather than blindly repeating them.

Creating Space for Self-Reflection

Capricorns might choose a quiet corner in their room or a calm spot outdoors for reflection. They can bring a notebook or keep a simple digital log. During this time, they focus on what went well and what did not. They might also think about their feelings or note new insights. The key is honesty without harshness. Instead of blaming themselves, they look for ways to adjust. Over time, regular self-reflection can become a healthy practice that keeps them aligned with their deeper values and aims.

Overcoming Habitual Workaholism

A common habit for Capricorns is working long hours without breaks. They may see rest as something they must earn, or they might feel they have too many duties to pause. This pattern can lead to tiredness or physical strain. Changing it may mean planning short rest periods throughout the day, or making sure to have at least one day off per week. While it might feel odd at first, Capricorns often find they return to work with sharper focus if they allow themselves true downtime.

Moderating Strictness in Personal Habits

Outside of work, Capricorns can also be strict about personal habits, like diets or exercise routines. If they slip, they might feel guilt. It is important to remember that lapses happen. What matters is returning to the routine steadily, rather than punishing themselves. They might also talk to a health or fitness professional who can guide them toward a balanced approach, ensuring they do not push too hard. Being kind to themselves can help them stick to good habits in the long run.

Handling Emotional Patterns

Emotional habits can be just as powerful as physical ones. Capricorns might bottle up feelings or avoid talking about stress. This can become a pattern that causes tension or sudden outbursts.

Breaking such a habit might involve learning to share small thoughts or worries with a friend or family member more often. Over time, these open conversations can lighten the emotional load. It takes practice to shift a habit of hiding emotions, but the result can be healthier relationships and reduced stress.

Setting Boundaries as a Habit

Some Capricorns find it hard to say "no," especially if they are used to taking on extra responsibilities. Learning to set boundaries can be life-changing. This might mean politely declining tasks that are not their job or telling a friend they cannot meet because they need rest. Though they might fear disappointing others, being honest about limits can protect them from burnout. Over time, people usually respect this honesty and learn that Capricorn's time is valuable.

Regularly Checking Motivation

A person's reason for starting a habit can change over time. For example, a Capricorn might begin a new study routine to improve in a subject. After a few months, they might realize they need that time for something else. Instead of continuing out of habit alone, they can check if the routine still supports their bigger aims. If not, it may be time to adapt or replace it with a habit that fits their current goals. This avoids wasting energy on actions that no longer serve them.

Spiritual or Mindful Practices

Not all Capricorns are into spiritual or mindful activities, but some discover that these practices help them. Whether it is a simple breathing exercise, calm reading before bed, or a gentle nature walk, these moments can quiet a busy mind. They do not have to be lengthy or complicated. A few minutes of mindful breathing each day can lower stress and keep them connected to the present. If they track how these practices affect their mood, they might see a real improvement in their overall comfort.

Designing an Environment That Supports Good Habits

Sometimes, changing habits is easier when the environment also changes. For instance, if a Capricorn wants to read more but never finds time, they could keep a book on their nightstand and decide on a set reading time. If they want to eat healthier, they can arrange their kitchen so fruits and vegetables are easier to reach than snacks. These small adjustments remove barriers, making it more likely they will stick with the new behavior. Capricorn's knack for organization can be a big help here.

Rewarding Good Habits

Though Capricorns can be serious, they still appreciate feeling good about hitting targets. They might set a simple reward after sticking with a habit for a certain number of days—like buying a helpful tool or enjoying a relaxed evening watching a favorite show. The reward should not sabotage their goals (for example, skipping an entire week of healthy eating), but it can be a small perk that keeps them motivated.

Avoiding All-or-Nothing Thinking

A Capricorn might slip into the mindset of "I must do my habit perfectly or not at all." This is a common trap. Life often disrupts routines. If they miss one day of their planned schedule, they do not have to abandon the entire habit. A more helpful approach is to accept that some days will not be perfect, but they can still continue the habit the next day. This gentle approach prevents them from losing long-term progress due to temporary interruptions.

Keeping Track of Changes

Capricorns love structure, so they might find it helpful to keep a habit tracker. This could be a paper checklist, a spreadsheet, or a simple phone app. For each day they follow through on their chosen behavior—like drinking enough water, walking for 20 minutes, or reading a helpful book—they mark it down. Over weeks, they see a chain of successes forming. This visual progress can feel satisfying, encouraging them to keep going.

Identifying Negative Habits

Not all habits are good. A Capricorn might overwork daily, avoid personal connections, or spend too much time thinking about mistakes. Recognizing these patterns is the first step. Then, they can decide how to replace them with healthier actions. For example, if they realize they are spending hours scrolling on their phone at night, they could set a limit or turn the phone off earlier. Instead, they might choose an activity that relaxes them but does not harm their rest.

Self-Reflection with Journaling

Journaling is a direct way to see how thoughts and behaviors connect. A Capricorn can write down what happened each day, how they felt, and whether they kept up with the habits they want. Over time, patterns might emerge—like noticing they skip their healthy routine when they have a stressful meeting. With this clarity, they can plan how to handle stress so it does not derail them. Journaling also provides a safe space to be open with themselves, which is especially useful if they usually keep feelings inside.

Learning from Setbacks

A setback is not a final defeat. If Capricorns see a habit slip—maybe they stop going to bed on time or skip exercise for a week—they can treat that as a signal. Perhaps something in their routine or mindset changed. By calmly analyzing the cause, they can adjust their plan or get needed help. A slip does not wipe out the progress they have made; it just shows that something needs to shift or improve. This forgiving attitude helps them return to their habits sooner instead of giving up in frustration.

Celebrating Tiny Wins

Capricorns do not usually boast about small successes. However, recognizing little steps can keep morale high. Maybe they managed to do a short exercise session even though the day was hectic. That is a step worth noting. They might say to themselves, "I kept my promise, even if it was only a short workout." This sense of satisfaction can push them to keep going. They do not have to throw a big party for every milestone. A simple nod to themselves or a note in a journal can be enough to build a positive mindset.

Habits for Emotional Well-Being

Beyond the physical sphere, Capricorns can create habits that tend to their emotional needs. This might include calling a close friend once a week, scheduling a short evening to watch a film with a loved one, or practicing a calming hobby. These habits guard against isolation and help them remember life is more than just tasks. Over time, these moments can deepen relationships and provide a feeling of support that a purely work-focused life might not give.

Adaptation Over Time

As Capricorns grow older or as their life situation shifts, the habits that once served them might need adjusting. For example, a habit of studying late at night might not work when they have to wake up early for a new job. Being open to these natural changes ensures they do not cling to routines that no longer fit. Instead, they can make new plans that align with their current reality, continuing to support their success and well-being.

Making Self-Reflection an Ongoing Habit

A single reflection is helpful, but making it regular can deeply shape a Capricorn's life. They might choose a monthly or quarterly check-in. During that time, they ask questions like:

- **Which habits still benefit me and align with my goals?**
- **Where am I struggling, and why?**
- **Do I need to add or remove any habit to stay balanced?**

They do not have to wait for problems to arise before making changes. This proactive attitude can prevent them from drifting too far from what they truly value.

Positive Role Models

Capricorns might look up to mentors or friends who have strong habits. Observing how these people keep a steady routine could offer ideas for their own life. They might also read biographies of persons who overcame challenges through self-discipline. These examples can show that sticking to good habits, combined with reflection, can lead to large achievements over time. However, they must also remember that each person's path is unique. They can adapt methods to fit their own personality and needs.

Balancing Alone Time and Social Habits

Some Capricorns can become so wrapped up in their daily structure that they forget to socialize. While alone time is vital for recharging, social connections are also part of healthy living. Making a habit of calling a friend or joining a small group activity once a week can maintain relationships. This might be part of their routine, just like any other important task. A sense of community can help Capricorns stay grounded and bring more joy into their life.

Growth Through Self-Honesty

Ultimately, habits and self-reflection mean little if a Capricorn is not honest with themselves. That honesty includes admitting when something is not working, when they need a break, or when a certain path is no longer right. It also includes accepting compliments or recognizing achievements without dismissing them. This balanced perspective helps them refine their actions. Over time, they can shape a life that meets both their practical side and their inner desires.

Conclusion: Nurturing Healthy Patterns

Habits give structure to Capricorn's day, making it easier for them to use their time wisely and pursue their aims. Self-reflection ensures those habits remain connected to what they genuinely need and value. By reviewing their progress, learning from mistakes, and celebrating small wins, Capricorns can maintain a strong sense of direction. They do not need a perfect system—just one that aligns with their steady style and respects the reality of life's ups and downs. In the end, well-chosen habits, combined with honest self-reflection, can empower Capricorns to live with purpose, balance, and a measure of calm fulfillment.

CHAPTER 15: CAPRICORN AND OTHER ZODIAC SIGNS

Why Compare Capricorn to Other Signs?

Each zodiac sign is said to have its own traits. People sometimes wonder how signs get along or clash. For Capricorn, its careful nature and steady approach might work nicely with certain signs, while it could create tensions with others. By seeing how these qualities mix or contrast, we can get hints about friendships, teamwork, or romantic bonds. While these insights are not strict rules, they can be fun or useful to think about.

Capricorn and Aries

- **Similarities:** Both can be determined and focused on plans. Aries has strong drive, and Capricorn has strong patience. They can finish tasks if they agree on a direction.

- **Differences:** Aries might rush ahead, wanting quick results, while Capricorn prefers step-by-step actions. Capricorn likes steady progress, and Aries likes fast progress. This might cause arguments if Aries pushes too hard or if Capricorn slows things down.

- **Advice:** They can learn from each other. Aries can show Capricorn how to be bolder. Capricorn can show Aries the benefits of patience. If they respect each other's pace, they might form a good team, with Aries supplying energy and Capricorn offering structure.

Capricorn and Taurus

- **Similarities:** Both are earth signs. They might share a liking for stable routines and practical goals. They value loyalty, so they can trust each other easily.

- **Differences:** Taurus can be easygoing about comfort, while Capricorn might be stricter about rules. Taurus might enjoy relaxing moments more, and Capricorn could think about work even during rest.

- **Advice:** They can build a steady, caring bond if they balance Taurus's wish for comfort with Capricorn's ambition. Taurus can remind Capricorn to pause sometimes, and Capricorn can help Taurus stick to important tasks.

Capricorn and Gemini

- **Similarities:** Both can be curious in their own ways—Gemini enjoys learning new facts, and Capricorn likes to master a topic step by step.

- **Differences:** Gemini might jump from idea to idea, enjoying variety. Capricorn prefers a clear plan and staying on one path until it is finished. Gemini could find Capricorn too rigid, and Capricorn might find Gemini too scattered.

- **Advice:** If they share tasks, Gemini can bring bright ideas, while Capricorn sets up a realistic plan. Clear communication helps. Gemini must respect Capricorn's cautious side, and Capricorn can accept that variety can spark creativity.

Capricorn and Cancer

- **Similarities:** They are opposite signs on the zodiac wheel, but they can share a desire for safety. Cancer wants emotional safety, while Capricorn wants real-world safety (like finances or career). Both care about long-term well-being.

- **Differences:** Cancer might rely on feelings to decide, while Capricorn leans on logic. Sometimes Capricorn appears cold to Cancer, and sometimes Cancer appears too sensitive to Capricorn.

- **Advice:** Both can support each other if they see the other's viewpoint. Cancer can show Capricorn the power of empathy, and Capricorn can show Cancer how planning reduces worry. They might form a balanced team if they talk openly about needs.

Capricorn and Leo

- **Similarities:** Both can be strong-willed. They want to do well, though Leo might crave attention and Capricorn might crave respect.

- **Differences:** Leo often likes the spotlight, while Capricorn likes to work quietly. Leo might see Capricorn as too strict, and Capricorn might see Leo as too dramatic.

- **Advice:** If they combine Capricorn's drive to get things done with Leo's ability to shine, they could achieve a lot. Each should acknowledge the other's strengths. Leo can bring warmth to Capricorn's serious approach, and Capricorn can keep Leo grounded.

Capricorn and Virgo

- **Similarities:** Both are earth signs. They typically prefer details and planning. They might share an interest in being organized or doing tasks well.

- **Differences:** Virgo might be more anxious or picky about small details. Capricorn is more concerned about the big goal and might overlook tiny points. Sometimes Virgo's worry can clash with Capricorn's bigger structure.

- **Advice:** They can create a strong, practical team if Virgo handles fine points and Capricorn leads the bigger plan. They both value clarity, so communication can be smooth as long as they respect each other's style.

Capricorn and Libra

- **Similarities:** Both can appreciate fairness. Capricorn likes clear rules, and Libra seeks harmony. They might enjoy polite discussions and balanced choices.

- **Differences:** Libra might have trouble making firm decisions, wanting everyone to be happy. Capricorn prefers to pick a path and stick to it. Libra might find Capricorn stiff, and Capricorn might find Libra hesitant.

- **Advice:** If Libra communicates feelings clearly, Capricorn can decide how to help. In return, Capricorn should be open to Libra's viewpoint about collaboration. Their bond can flourish if they both make sure that logic and fairness guide them in the same direction.

Capricorn and Scorpio

- **Similarities:** Both are careful about trusting others. They might test people before showing deeper parts of themselves. They can share a strong sense of purpose when they really want something.

- **Differences:** Scorpio might have intense emotions hidden underneath a calm face. Capricorn also keeps emotions private, but can seem more practical than emotional. Scorpio might want deeper emotional exchanges, while Capricorn stays more logical.

- **Advice:** Their shared cautious style can give them respect for each other. Scorpio can learn from Capricorn's steady approach, and Capricorn can learn from Scorpio's powerful focus on emotional insight. If they open up gradually, they can form a strong, loyal bond.

Capricorn and Sagittarius

- **Similarities:** Both can be goal-oriented. They like seeing results. Sagittarius may focus on wide experiences, while Capricorn wants measurable results.

- **Differences:** Sagittarius loves freedom and might resist too many plans. Capricorn loves planning and might think Sagittarius is too impulsive. Sometimes Sagittarius wants to explore different options, while Capricorn wants to stick to a chosen path.

- **Advice:** They can learn from each other's methods. Sagittarius can show Capricorn how trying new approaches can lead to growth, and Capricorn can show Sagittarius the rewards of persistence. They should talk about shared aims and keep each other updated on changes.

Capricorn and Capricorn

- **Similarities:** Two Capricorns can create a very stable pair—both plan carefully, keep promises, and strive for steady success. They might understand each other's seriousness.

- **Differences:** They could compete over who controls the plan if they are not careful. They might also become too strict, with no one adding fun.

- **Advice:** They can be a power team if they agree on goals and remember to allow fun or emotional openness. Since both can be reserved, they need to watch out for unspoken feelings. Mutual respect can be strong, but a bit of lightness keeps them from feeling heavy.

Capricorn and Aquarius

- **Similarities:** Both can be thoughtful. Capricorn thinks about practical structure, and Aquarius thinks about bigger ideas for society or progress. They can admire each other's intellect.

- **Differences:** Aquarius might find Capricorn too focused on traditions, while Capricorn might find Aquarius too unconventional. Aquarius may not want to follow rules unless they make sense, and Capricorn sees value in rules for order.

- **Advice:** They can combine Capricorn's plan-making skills with Aquarius's innovative ideas. As long as Capricorn stays open to fresh concepts, and Aquarius respects the need for some structure, they can work well together. Each side benefits if they explain their reasons fully.

Capricorn and Pisces

- **Similarities:** Both can be gentle in their own way. Capricorn is gentle with actions, Pisces is gentle with feelings. They might unite around caring for loved ones or meeting needs.

- **Differences:** Pisces tends to dream and feel deeply, sometimes forgetting real-world limits. Capricorn is all about practicality. Pisces might see Capricorn as too strict, while Capricorn might see Pisces as too naive.

- **Advice:** If Pisces brings empathy and creative thinking, and Capricorn provides structure, they can complement each other. Capricorn can help turn Pisces's ideas into real steps. Pisces can remind Capricorn that sometimes imagination and kindness are just as important as logic.

Working Together with Different Signs

In a team setting, Capricorns pair well with signs that appreciate planning or stable progress. Earth signs (Taurus, Virgo, Capricorn) often share similar working styles. Water signs (Cancer, Scorpio, Pisces) can bring emotional depth, which might balance Capricorn's logical side. Fire signs (Aries, Leo, Sagittarius) bring excitement, which can spark new ideas, but might also clash if Capricorn feels rushed. Air signs (Gemini, Libra, Aquarius) bring fresh perspectives, though Capricorn might feel they change directions too fast. With open communication, these differences can enrich rather than divide.

Social or Friendship Bonds

In casual friendships, Capricorn might gravitate toward those who respect boundaries and do not push for constant excitement. That means stable signs like Taurus or Virgo can be natural fits. However, a friend like Aries or Leo might pull Capricorn into fun activities they would not try alone. Libra or Gemini friends could provide lightness in conversations. Scorpio or Cancer friends might share deeper personal talks. Each match can work if there is mutual understanding.

Romantic Compatibility

In romantic ties, it is not only about sun signs. A person's full birth chart matters, but people often look to the main zodiac sign for hints. Capricorn might find comfort with Taurus or Virgo, who share practical traits. Cancer can provide warmth, and Scorpio can bring intensity. Pisces might offer a gentle emotional space. Aries or Leo might need to adjust a bit more to handle Capricorn's cautious style. Any pair can work if both parties learn to meet in the middle.

Learning from Contrasts

Where differences appear, they can spark growth if both sides are respectful. A Capricorn might feel frustrated by someone's spontaneity, but that same spontaneity can bring fresh ideas. On the flip side, a lively sign might find Capricorn's caution tedious, but it can also lead to strong planning that benefits everyone. When signs accept that each style has worth, they can create a healthy balance of energies.

Communication Tips Across the Zodiac

- **With Fire Signs (Aries, Leo, Sagittarius):** Remain open to their bursts of enthusiasm. They appreciate direct feedback but do not smother their spark.

- **With Earth Signs (Taurus, Virgo, Capricorn):** Use shared practicality to keep tasks organized. Avoid being too stubborn; remain flexible.

- **With Air Signs (Gemini, Libra, Aquarius):** Listen to their ideas, even if they seem scattered at first. Offer a plan to ground those thoughts.

- **With Water Signs (Cancer, Scorpio, Pisces):** Show some empathy. Their feelings might run deep, so be patient and try to understand the emotional viewpoint.

Handling Conflicts

In any sign pairing, conflicts happen. Capricorn might try to solve problems logically, which not all signs appreciate. If the other sign is highly emotional, Capricorn can learn to listen without rushing straight to solutions. If the other sign is impulsive, Capricorn can calmly explain reasons for caution instead of shutting them down. Mutual respect helps each side feel heard. Clear communication and a willingness to compromise can prevent small disagreements from becoming bigger than they need to be.

When Different Styles Combine

Even if two signs seem unlikely to match, they can find common ground. A fiery sign can motivate Capricorn. A watery sign can add feelings that Capricorn sometimes hides. An airy sign can provide new angles, and an earthy sign can share Capricorn's steadiness. Each sign has something special to offer, and Capricorn's methodical approach can support or anchor the connection.

Remembering Individual Differences

It is key to note that no zodiac pair is guaranteed to succeed or fail. A person's upbringing, personal experiences, and full birth chart shape who they are. Some Capricorns might be very outgoing, while others are shy. The same is true for every sign. These observations are just broad patterns. Real compatibility depends on willingness to listen, learn, and adapt.

Growing Together

Capricorns are often ready to grow within relationships—be they friendly, professional, or romantic—if they see it makes sense. They prefer not to waste time on endless drama. When they meet signs who seem chaotic, they might try to introduce some order or show the benefits of planning. In turn, they can let go of some of their rigidity to see that a bit of spontaneity or emotional depth can make life richer.

Stronger Connections

By knowing how Capricorn's style might mix or clash with others, people can handle differences more gracefully. Capricorn can develop strategies for each sign, such as keeping calm with an impulsive Aries, or providing thoughtful reassurance to a sensitive Cancer. At the same time, others can learn to appreciate Capricorn's methodical steps and not see them as stubbornness. Common understanding can lead to friendships or working relationships that last.

Using Zodiac Insights Wisely

While these ideas can be fun, it is wise not to box people into labels. If a Capricorn meets a Gemini, they should not assume the union is doomed just because they have different speeds. Instead, they can use the tips above: talk clearly, balance logic with fun, and be open to learning from each other. That way, the zodiac can act as a guide rather than a final verdict.

Shared Projects or Goals

If Capricorn joins forces with other signs in a project, they can notice how each sign adds value. For example, an air sign might excel at brainstorming, a fire sign might handle quick actions, a water sign might support group morale, and an earth sign might keep tasks on track. Recognizing each sign's gift helps Capricorn lead or join a diverse team effectively. It also prevents frustration since each person is allowed to work in their own best way.

Finding Joy in Differences

Instead of seeing conflicting traits as problems, Capricorns can see them as ways to expand their own viewpoint. An enthusiastic sign can bring joy to a Capricorn's serious routine. A dreamy sign might help Capricorn explore new possibilities. Meanwhile, Capricorn's stability can be a calming force for those who are easily carried away by emotion or excitement. When differences are welcomed, everyone benefits.

Last Thoughts on Compatibility

No sign is perfect for Capricorn, and no sign is completely incompatible. It is about how people handle each other's quirks and approaches to life. Communication, patience, and kindness can bridge many gaps. Whether working in a team, forming friendships, or exploring romance, knowing these broad patterns can help Capricorn see areas of potential strength or conflict right from the start.

Conclusion

Capricorn relates to each sign differently, shaped by shared traits or distinct traits. Understanding these common themes can offer a glimpse into how Capricorn might cooperate or clash with others. By staying open-minded, using clear communication, and balancing logic with empathy, Capricorn can form relationships that support their steady nature while also inviting growth. Every connection, whether with an earth sign or a fire sign, can teach Capricorn something new, helping them refine their view of the world and the people in it.

CHAPTER 16: CAPRICORN THROUGH DIFFERENT AGES

Why Look at Different Life Stages?

We change as we get older, and Capricorns can show their typical traits in ways that fit each age. A Capricorn child might act more mature than expected. A Capricorn teenager might already be thinking about the future. A Capricorn adult may become quite focused on career or family responsibilities. By looking at these stages, we can see how Capricorn's basic nature remains, yet also adapts as life moves forward.

Capricorn as a Child

- **Observing the World:** Even when very young, Capricorn children often watch what is happening around them. They might seem quieter or more serious than other kids. They could be careful in play, testing how toys work rather than rushing in.

- **Early Responsibility:** Some Capricorn children enjoy helping with small chores. They might feel proud when they do something grown-up, like organizing toys or following a simple task list. Parents might notice they prefer structure, such as a regular bedtime or meal routine.

- **Need for Encouragement:** Because they can be serious, they might put pressure on themselves early. Adults can remind them that mistakes are normal. Offering gentle praise for effort, not just results, can help them feel more at ease.

Capricorn in Late Childhood

- **Building Confidence:** As they enter school age, Capricorn kids often like tasks that let them see steady progress (like a reading log, a project, or a collection). They might enjoy accomplishing steps and checking things off a list.

- **Reliable Helpers:** Teachers might appreciate how Capricorn children show up on time, follow instructions, or complete homework carefully. These kids might take it to heart if they let a teacher down, so they can be sensitive to criticism.

- **Play and Learning:** While they might do well academically, they also need room to have fun. If they become too serious, they can miss out on creative play. Encouraging them to try new games, sports, or art can help them keep a healthy balance.

Capricorn as a Teen

- **Early Future Thinking:** Capricorn teens may already be thinking about college, training, or future jobs. They could talk about career paths while peers are just focusing on present interests. This drive can help them excel, but it can also add stress.

- **Social Life:** Capricorn teenagers might be picky about friends. They could bond with classmates who share their sense of responsibility. They might avoid big group events if they feel they have no clear purpose. At the same time, finding a few reliable friends gives them a sense of belonging.

- **Rebellion or Caution?** Some teens rebel by breaking rules. Capricorns might rebel in quieter ways—like setting their own study methods or ignoring trends they see as pointless. Others might stick closely to rules, wanting to avoid conflict. Either way, they often want to feel in control of their path.

Balancing School and Personal Interests

- **Study Habits:** Capricorns usually form strong study routines. They might organize notes, create flashcards, or follow a strict schedule. This can lead to good grades. But if they fixate on perfection, they risk feeling anxious when the workload is heavy.

- **Finding Hobbies:** Alongside academic goals, it is important that Capricorn teens explore interests for fun. Whether it is music, art, or sports, having a break from constant study can refresh their mind. Parents and teachers can gently encourage them to step away from homework now and then.

Capricorn in Early Adulthood

- **Entering the Workforce or Higher Education:** After finishing school, many Capricorns are eager to join the adult world. They might choose a practical college major or a job that offers room for growth. They may not mind starting at an entry level, as long as they see a clear ladder to climb.

- **Focus on Stability:** Young adult Capricorns might begin to save money early. They could plan for a car, a place to live, or other important investments. They might also set their sights on a promotion or a specific role, building up experience step by step.

- **Social Shifts:** While some peers might want to travel or try different lifestyles, Capricorn might stick to a stable routine.

This can cause them to feel out of place among adventurous friends. Finding a circle that respects their ambitions can help.

Building a Career Path

- **Steady Progress:** In their 20s and 30s, Capricorns often focus on establishing a strong career. They might accept extra tasks to show their skills or stay late to perfect details. Their sense of duty can impress bosses or clients.

- **Leadership Potential:** Over time, Capricorns might move into management roles because they handle tasks and people with calm authority. They like fair rules and can create a structured environment. However, they should watch out for becoming too rigid.

- **Money Management:** This is often when a Capricorn's financial planning starts to bear fruit. They might purchase a home or build a solid retirement fund. They prefer slow, consistent financial growth.

Capricorn in Personal Relationships

- **Choosing a Partner:** In their 20s or 30s, Capricorns may look for a partner who shares similar values—loyalty, responsibility, and a focus on the future. They do not usually jump into serious commitments overnight.

- **Balancing Love and Work:** It can be tricky for Capricorns to make time for emotional closeness if they are busy building a career. Partners might feel neglected if Capricorn forgets to relax and connect. Making room for quality time can protect the relationship.

- **Starting a Family (If They Choose To):** If Capricorn becomes a parent, they might show the same careful approach: researching parenting methods, setting routines for kids, and teaching values like effort and respect. Still, they must remember that children need free play and open emotion, not just structure.

Midlife: Shifting Priorities

- **Reaching Goals:** In middle age, Capricorns might have hit many of their early career targets. They could have a comfortable position and a stable home. Now they might look around and ask, "What next?" This can lead to exploring new hobbies or focusing on health.

- **Family and Community:** They may spend more time guiding younger relatives or volunteering. Their sense of duty might expand beyond personal goals to helping neighbors or local groups.

- **Handling Stress:** If a Capricorn spent decades working too hard, they could feel the strain now. Recognizing stress signals and learning to delegate can help them avoid burnout. This stage is a good time to build a healthier work-life balance if they did not do so before.

Reflecting on Achievements

- **Feeling Accomplished:** Capricorns who managed their careers and finances carefully can enjoy a sense of security. They might own their home, have steady savings, or hold a respected position. This can bring pride and relief.

- **Possible Midlife Crisis:** On the other hand, some Capricorns might worry they focused too much on tasks and not enough on personal happiness. They might look for new directions—like a hobby, a new career, or more family bonding. Being open to change can keep this from becoming a crisis.

Capricorn in Later Years

- **Shifting to Mentor Role:** As Capricorns grow older, they often become seen as wise or experienced by younger people at work or in the family. They can share knowledge about managing resources, making practical plans, or persevering through challenges.

- **Enjoying the Fruits of Labor:** If they planned finances well, they can afford a comfortable retirement. Some continue a part-time role or run a small project to stay active. They enjoy a quiet life, often preferring calm routines.

- **Emotional Rewards:** Over time, Capricorn might soften. They realize strictness is not the only key to a rich life. Grandchildren or community involvement can open a more nurturing side that was less visible in earlier years.

Common Pitfalls at Each Stage

- **Childhood:** Might feel pressure to be "the good kid" or try too hard to be perfect. Needs freedom to play.

- **Teen Years:** Could become overly focused on grades or future plans, missing normal teenage fun. Needs reminders that balance is healthy.

- **Early Adulthood:** Risks working nonstop and neglecting relationships or self-care. Needs to pace themselves.

- **Midlife:** Might face health issues if they have pushed themselves too long. Needs to incorporate rest and reflect on personal fulfillment.

- **Later Years:** Could become lonely if they have not built emotional ties. Needs to share wisdom and connect with loved ones.

Adapting at Each Phase

Capricorns can handle change better when they plan for it. For example, a teen can plan for college finances well before graduation. A new parent can read about healthy ways to handle stress. A middle-aged Capricorn can gradually cut back work hours instead of retiring abruptly. By seeing transitions coming, they can shift slowly, which suits their cautious nature.

Emotional Growth Over Time

- **Child to Teen:** A Capricorn learns that not everything can be controlled. They adapt to new subjects, social circles, and responsibilities.

- **Teen to Adult:** They realize that genuine success comes from balancing ambition with self-care. They also learn that building real friendships or love takes more than just focusing on tasks.

- **Adult to Elder Years:** They discover that a well-rounded life includes relationships, hobbies, and giving back. Ambition remains, but they might measure success by lasting impact rather than just job titles.

Changing Views on Success

Early in life, Capricorn might define success as achieving a certain rank or salary. Over time, they could see that success also involves health, relationships, and inner peace. This growth can encourage them to broaden their goals, aiming not just for professional achievements but also for meaningful personal experiences. They learn that a secure retirement can be lonely if they never built emotional connections.

Role of Mentors and Guides

Each life stage can be eased if Capricorns have patient mentors. A teacher, boss, or older friend can show them that it is okay to make mistakes, explore new paths, or rest. Because Capricorns respect experience, such mentors can teach them skills and mindsets to manage transitions. Later, Capricorns often become mentors themselves, passing on the lessons they learned.

Staying Flexible Over the Years

Some Capricorns might cling to the same methods at 50 that they used at 20. This can lead to frustration in a changing world. If they stay open to new tech, new ways of working, or new ideas, they can remain relevant and engaged. This does not mean ditching all traditions. Instead, it means mixing classic Capricorn reliability with the ability to adapt. For instance, a older Capricorn might learn to use digital tools for their finances or keep in touch with family through video calls.

Relationships Through Ages

- **Friendships:** Childhood friends might remain if they share Capricorn's loyal nature. In adult years, friendships might focus on common interests like parenting, work, or hobbies. In later years, companionship and shared memories might become more precious.

- **Romance:** Early relationships could be cautious. Over time, Capricorn might become more comfortable showing affection if they trust a partner. A long-term bond can deepen through shared plans and stable progress.

- **Family:** If Capricorn has children, they often teach them about responsibility and planning. Grandchildren can bring a gentle side. If they do not have children, they might direct their caring energy toward nieces, nephews, or community roles.

Health Awareness with Age

- **Childhood:** Busy building bones and learning routines. Good for them to stay active in play.

- **Teen and Young Adult:** Might adopt strong exercise or study habits. Need to watch for stress.

- **Midlife:** Should check for signs of overwork, paying attention to heart health or stress levels.

- **Later Years:** Regular checkups, gentle physical activity, and balanced nutrition become even more important. Capricorn's habit of scheduling can help them keep up with medical visits and stay on top of small health concerns before they grow.

Career Changes

Not all Capricorns stick to one path. Some might shift careers if they see a better opportunity. They can be quite practical about this, researching the pros and cons. In midlife, they might realize they want a job with more meaning rather than just a high salary. If they do switch, they plan carefully, often taking courses or building new skills before jumping in. This measured approach helps them adapt with less risk.

Balancing Legacy and Enjoyment

As they reach the later stages, Capricorns might ask themselves what they want to leave behind. This could be a stable company, a family tradition, or a community project. They might also want to enjoy hobbies or travel (if they choose) while they still can. By mixing these aims, they can find satisfaction. They keep shaping their environment while also savoring the rewards of their many years of effort.

Embracing Community

Throughout the years, Capricorns often learn that teamwork and community are valuable. Joining a local club, volunteering, or connecting with neighbors can fill a social need they might have ignored when younger. They might share their planning skills with a group, or help organize events. This can bring a sense of belonging and a feeling of purpose beyond personal achievements.

Adapting to Retirement

At retirement, some Capricorns feel lost if they do not have a job to anchor their day. They might fear boredom or a lack of structure. To handle this, they can create a retirement routine. Maybe they take morning walks, join a group class, or dedicate time to a cause. They can also keep a hobby that uses their skills—like consulting or teaching. This way, they remain mentally active and socially involved.

Lifetime Lessons

Through all stages, Capricorns discover that success alone does not guarantee happiness. While ambition and practical planning bring security, close ties and emotional warmth bring deeper satisfaction. Striking that balance can be the most important lesson. Over a lifetime, they develop from cautious children to wise, steady elders who can share insights about resilience, loyalty, and the rewards of patient effort.

Allowing Growth at Every Phase

It is never too late for a Capricorn to adjust habits or try new experiences. Even in senior years, they might learn a new skill or connect with different groups. Each age brings its own challenges, but Capricorn's perseverance can guide them through. A child might learn to loosen up, a teen might explore interests, an adult might switch careers, and a senior might find new ways to stay active. Each stage is a chance to refine their stable, caring style.

Supporting Capricorn's Growth

Friends and family can help Capricorns at each age by respecting their careful nature while gently encouraging them to explore. Simple praises, sincere offers of help, or honest conversations can make them feel supported. If they sense that loved ones understand their drive and also care about their well-being, they are more likely to trust and open up. This helps them handle life's turns without feeling alone.

Common Threads Across Life

No matter the age, most Capricorns value hard work, practicality, and loyalty. In childhood, this might mean sharing toys fairly. In teen years, it might mean meeting responsibilities at home and school. In adulthood, it can show through steady career moves. In later life, it might appear as reliability for family and community. These traits remain, but how they are expressed can shift with the person's changing roles and goals.

Chapter Conclusion

Capricorn's qualities—like patience, responsibility, and a sense of structure—stay present across the years. As a child, they might appear as the quiet one who follows rules. In the teen years, they plan ahead more than others. In young adulthood, they focus on building a strong base for work or finances. In midlife, they seek balance and reflect on what truly matters. In later life, they often turn into wise mentors who appreciate the results of a carefully built life. Through these stages, a willingness to adapt, stay aware of emotional needs, and share knowledge helps Capricorn find lasting fulfillment.

CHAPTER 17: COMMON BELIEFS AROUND CAPRICORN

Overview of Beliefs and Stereotypes
Over many centuries, people have formed various ideas about Capricorn. Some see Capricorn as a serious or even severe zodiac sign, assuming that individuals born under it are always stern and never have fun. Others believe that Capricorns are cold-hearted or overly ambitious. Of course, broad labels do not apply to everyone. Real people are more complex. Still, these ideas can shape how others view Capricorns and how Capricorns come to see themselves.

Roots of These Beliefs
Many beliefs come from Capricorn's link with Saturn, a planet that astrologers often link to lessons, time, and structure. Because Saturn is seen as strict, some believe Capricorn always acts like an older figure who enforces rules and punishes mistakes. Historically, Capricorn season comes in winter in many parts of the world, a time that can appear cold or barren. This might add to the idea that Capricorn is harsh or somber. However, as with any symbol, these are just associations that might not reflect everyone's real personality.

"Capricorns Never Have Fun"
One common belief is that Capricorns do not like laughter or relaxation. It is true that many Capricorns can be quiet or cautious. They might also hold themselves to high standards, which could seem serious. But that does not mean they dislike fun. They may simply choose calmer or more meaningful forms of enjoyment, such as a hobby they can plan or a relaxing night with close friends. They tend to avoid rowdy events or sudden chaos. Rather than disliking

fun, they might just prefer to feel prepared and comfortable before letting go.

"Capricorns Are Always Cold and Unemotional"

Another idea says that Capricorn is too logical to feel emotions deeply. In reality, Capricorns often feel plenty of emotions. They might not show them as clearly, preferring to handle them in private. Some Capricorns are even quite warm, especially with those they trust. The habit of holding back feelings can come from a desire to avoid vulnerability or a worry that big emotional displays might disrupt order. This does not mean the emotions are not there; they are simply managed in a quieter way.

"All Capricorns Care About Is Work"

Since many Capricorns set long-term goals and work carefully toward them, onlookers might say they are obsessed with their jobs or careers. It is true that a Capricorn might choose to stay late at work or study extra for a class. However, it is not always about job titles or money. Often, they want to feel secure and see that their time is used well. They might also enjoy the sense of accomplishment that comes from a completed task. Some Capricorns might pour similar energy into hobbies, volunteer work, or other pursuits that are not job-related at all.

"Capricorns Cannot Be Creative"

Because Capricorns value practical thinking, they are sometimes labeled as lacking creativity. But there are many Capricorns who excel in music, art, writing, or other creative fields. They might approach these areas with the same methodical mindset they use for everything else: planning, practicing, and refining their craft. Creativity can take different shapes. For a Capricorn, it might show up as building a structured story, designing a new system for art supplies, or steadily perfecting a musical skill over time.

"They Are Too Bossy or Controlling"

Some people say Capricorns always want to be in charge. This might come from seeing a Capricorn organize tasks or point out the best method. While it is true that many Capricorns enjoy leading or shaping a project, that does not always mean they desire power for its own sake. Often, they take on leadership because they feel they can maintain stability or guide a group effectively. If they are in an environment with fair leadership already, they may not feel the need to step in. If they seem controlling, it might be from wanting things done well rather than a wish to dominate.

"They Are Overly Traditional or Outdated"

Capricorn's reputation for liking structure can lead to the assumption that they reject anything new. Some do prefer long-standing routines or methods, seeing them as proven over time. However, many Capricorns are open to modern ideas if those ideas clearly work. They may not jump onto every trend, but they can adapt when they see real benefits. They balance tradition with practicality, discarding old ways that no longer fit while keeping useful ones. This cautious approach can stop them from chasing fads that might fade quickly.

Misreading Capricorn's Boundaries

Capricorns often have personal boundaries that others might mistake for indifference. For example, a Capricorn might politely keep personal details to themselves until they feel safe sharing. Some interpret this as aloofness. In reality, many Capricorns want meaningful connections, but they also want to ensure trust. They might need more time to reveal their inner world. Once comfortable, they can be loyal friends or partners who show thoughtfulness and kindness.

Historic Beliefs About Capricorn

In ancient times, Capricorn was seen as a sign of the winter solstice (in the Northern Hemisphere). This was a turning point from longer nights back to growing daylight. Some historical beliefs said Capricorn people have an inner wisdom, linked to the idea of enduring cold, dark times. This could explain the notion that they are cautious and serious. Over many centuries, these associations became part of the image of Capricorn, but they do not define every individual.

Modern Media Portrayals

In movies or books, if a character is described as a Capricorn, they might be shown as an ambitious professional, always aiming for the top. They might also be depicted as strict or unyielding. These portrayals can reinforce stereotypes. Although sometimes there is truth in how a Capricorn character is shown, it usually only reveals a narrow slice of how Capricorn traits can manifest in real people.

Positive Beliefs

There are also uplifting beliefs about Capricorn. People might say Capricorns are highly dependable, solid friends, and good at managing resources. They may be seen as the "rock" that keeps things from falling apart. These beliefs highlight qualities like loyalty, strength, and perseverance. While such compliments can be encouraging, Capricorns might feel pressure to always be the stable one, even when they need support themselves.

Cultural Differences

In some places, people pay more attention to zodiac signs, while in others, it might be a small interest. The beliefs about Capricorn can also vary by culture. For instance, some cultures associate the goat or sea goat with wisdom or cunning. Others might link Saturn with a more forbidding or teacher-like presence. Because these cultural angles differ, a Capricorn's family or social environment can shape how they see their own sign and how others treat them.

Combating Negative Myths

For a Capricorn who feels weighed down by stereotypes, it might help to show their emotional side to close friends. They can also talk openly about interests that have nothing to do with work or money, reminding people that they are multifaceted. If confronted with statements like, "You are so dull because you are a Capricorn," they can gently explain or demonstrate that they have a fun side. Over time, personal actions can dissolve inaccurate beliefs.

Keeping a Sense of Humor

Some Capricorns find it amusing when people assume they never smile. They might respond with a playful comment or a small grin, showing they are not as cold as others think. Having a sense of humor about these beliefs can take away any sting. A Capricorn can prove that a serious approach does not equal a boring personality. In fact, many Capricorns enjoy witty or clever humor, appreciating jokes that have a bit of logic or insight behind them.

Astrology vs. Individual Variation

Astrology is a broad framework, and it does not determine every trait. Even two Capricorns with similar birth dates can differ a lot because of personal upbringing, life events, and unique personality quirks. While some parts of the stereotypes might fit certain Capricorns, others might behave in an entirely different way. Real personality is shaped by many factors, so it is wise not to rely too heavily on blanket beliefs.

Common Misinterpretations in Relationships

In a relationship, a partner might believe the Capricorn does not truly love them if they do not show grand gestures. But Capricorn often proves affection through loyal acts or by creating a secure environment. This difference in showing care can lead to misunderstandings. Another partner might think Capricorn only cares about success, not realizing that the Capricorn's goals also support the family's comfort or future. Talking openly can help clear up these mistaken views.

Capricorns and the Myth of "Complete Self-Reliance"

People sometimes think Capricorns do not need anyone else's help because they appear so steady. This can lead to the belief that Capricorns do not want or appreciate support. The reality is that many Capricorns do enjoy teamwork, companionship, and emotional bonds. They might not always ask for help, but they often value it when offered sincerely. Being seen as super self-sufficient can feel isolating if no one realizes they also need friendship or empathy.

Influence of Modern Media on Beliefs

With the internet and social media, zodiac-themed content is everywhere. Memes or short posts might reduce Capricorn traits to a handful of lines: "Always working," "No sense of humor," or "Has no emotions." These can spread quickly. While they might be fun or silly, they can cause people to judge a Capricorn before truly knowing them. Capricorns who feel misrepresented might correct friends by sharing deeper insights or real examples from life.

Exploring Spiritual or Superstitious Views

In some spiritual communities, Capricorn is linked with discipline and mastery. People might see it as a sign that excels in tasks requiring concentration. There might also be superstitions—for instance, believing Capricorns need certain lucky charms or that they always face tough tests from fate due to Saturn's influence. Some Capricorns embrace these ideas if they find meaning in them, while others see them as fun myths to read about without taking them seriously.

Recognizing the Value of Grounded Traits

While some negative beliefs paint Capricorn as dull, the more balanced viewpoint is that Capricorn's grounded nature can be a real strength in a world full of changes. Their steady approach can help them build trust with peers, guide groups through uncertainty, and handle crises without panic. Over time, many come to appreciate the Capricorn style, even if it seemed too reserved at first glance.

Adapting to Changing Times

As society evolves, beliefs might shift too. Older stereotypes might fade, or new ones might form. Capricorns who adapt to modern needs—like technology, flexible work, or collaborative leadership—can show that they are not stuck in tradition. They keep their strong sense of responsibility while learning fresh methods. This mixture of tradition and modern thinking counters the idea that Capricorn cannot handle change.

Personal Responsibility vs. Astrological Labels

Some Capricorns might use their sign as a reason for certain behavior, saying, "I cannot be more open because I am a Capricorn." However, personal growth often requires looking beyond labels. If a Capricorn wants to show more emotion, they can practice, no matter what the stereotypes say. In the end, each person can decide how to shape their character rather than relying on broad beliefs.

Encouraging Positive Views

When friends, family, or coworkers talk about Capricorn, a Capricorn might take the chance to highlight real traits: reliability, loyalty, methodical thinking, and quiet support. By speaking about their genuine experiences, they can guide the conversation away from shallow labels. Over time, this can help others form a more balanced view of the sign.

Social Settings and Group Dynamics

In a party or group, others might not expect Capricorn to be the one who keeps track of items, ensures everyone is safe, or solves small problems behind the scenes. But these hidden contributions can be quite valuable. Recognizing that Capricorns often show care through actions (rather than big words) can clear up the belief that they are disinterested. They do care—they might just express it by doing, not by shouting it out.

Myths Within the Capricorn Community

Capricorns themselves can develop beliefs about their own sign, such as thinking they must always stay strong or never reveal emotions because that is "how a Capricorn should be." This can limit personal growth. Realizing that zodiac signs offer potential traits but do not force a single way of behaving can free Capricorns to explore other sides of themselves without guilt.

Looking Forward

As more people learn that astrology is just one lens for personality, some of the extreme beliefs may soften. Individuals can see Capricorns as people with a strong sense of duty, but also capable of warmth and creativity. Capricorns, in turn, can share their viewpoints with those who might believe only the stereotypes. Communication helps both sides see that behind the label is a person with a range of feelings, needs, and interests.

CHAPTER 18: CAPRICORN IN SOCIETY AND CULTURE

Role of Capricorn Traits in Broader Society

Capricorns often stand out in a community for their organized style and sense of responsibility. At times, society needs individuals who can keep track of details, set up systems, and see tasks through to completion. Because Capricorns tend to think long-term, they can assist groups in planning ahead. This applies to many areas—business, government, neighborhood committees, or volunteer programs. Their cautious approach helps keep projects realistic, and their careful monitoring can prevent missed deadlines or waste.

Contribution to Group Activities

Even in smaller social settings, such as hobby clubs or neighborhood gatherings, Capricorns might naturally fall into roles like treasurer, secretary, or event planner. They ensure that resources are used properly and that everyone knows their responsibilities. While not always the loudest voice in the room, the Capricorn's ability to bring order can create a stable foundation. If they are not the official leader, they might still offer behind-the-scenes support, helping the group stay on track.

Representation in Different Industries

- **Finance and Banking:** Capricorns can thrive in roles that handle money or budgets. Their knack for saving and avoiding big risks fits well in this environment.

- **Law and Administration:** Detailed thinking and a respect for rules can guide them toward successful work in law, government offices, or structured fields.

- **Entrepreneurship:** Some Capricorns start businesses, as they are often ready to put in the time and effort. Their approach might be careful, but it can lead to stable progress.

- **Creative Fields:** Although people might not expect it, Capricorns can do well in creative roles if they treat them as a craft, practicing and refining their work steadily. They might become skilled musicians, designers, or writers, focusing on quality over flashy speed.

Societal Expectations

Because of common stereotypes, society might see Capricorns as reliable workers who accept responsibilities without much complaint. At times, organizations might rely too heavily on them, assuming they will handle extra tasks. While Capricorns often do so effectively, they can burn out if they never feel recognized or if too much is placed on their shoulders. It is important for a Capricorn to set boundaries, even when society expects them to just keep going.

Historical Leaders and Figures

Looking back, there have been notable Capricorns in positions of power—such as political leaders, CEOs, or movement organizers. Their achievements often reflect the Capricorn style of patience, structure, and a consistent vision. However, these figures are more than just their zodiac sign. They also had personal experiences and resources that shaped their paths. Still, people sometimes point to these examples as proof that Capricorns can handle big responsibilities.

Cultural Symbols and Art

The sea goat symbol for Capricorn appears in various artworks, ancient seals, or astrology charts. In some cultures, goats have been symbols of endurance or sure-footedness, climbing steep hills to reach the top. The fish tail element in the traditional Capricorn symbol hints at emotional depth or hidden creativity. These cultural images can spark the imagination. Some artists might paint or sculpt a sea goat to represent the blend of practical and emotional sides present in many people.

Media Depictions

In TV shows or movies, a Capricorn character might be cast as the serious organizer, the responsible older sibling, or the methodical detective. They often bring stability to the plot, working behind the scenes or providing solutions. Sometimes, they are used as a foil to a more impulsive character, highlighting how their steady approach contrasts with a chaotic style. Though these portrayals might only scratch the surface, they do reflect society's view that Capricorn stands for order and persistence.

Influence in Educational Settings

In schools, Capricorn students might join or lead academic clubs. They might be class representatives or club treasurers, given their sense of duty. As adults, some Capricorns become teachers or professors. They might plan detailed syllabi and grading systems, creating clear goals for their students. This can bring a sense of security to the classroom, though it might also feel strict at times. Still, many students appreciate the clear direction, knowing exactly what is required to succeed.

Volunteer Work and Public Service

Many Capricorns put their skills toward volunteering, especially if they see a concrete way to help a cause. They might handle the finances of a charity or organize donation drives. Their attention to detail ensures that resources get where they need to go. This practical contribution can have a huge positive impact. On the other hand, Capricorns must be cautious not to take on every responsibility alone. Delegating tasks within volunteer groups can build more sustainable support for the cause.

Navigating Social Movements

If a Capricorn gets involved in social or political movements, they might focus on long-term strategies. While others might gather large crowds quickly, Capricorn might develop a plan for lasting reform. They could draft proposals, track data, or manage budgets. Although they might not always be the loudest protesters, they can strengthen the movement by keeping it organized. Their calm stance can also help during negotiations or when a cause needs a clear and detailed argument.

Capricorn's Standpoint on Technology

Some Capricorns embrace new tools if they see a real advantage—like software that streamlines tasks or apps that help budgeting. They might be slower to adopt flashy gadgets with no clear purpose. In broader society, this balanced approach can prevent wasteful spending or hype-driven choices. Capricorns often demand practical proof that a technology will improve efficiency before investing time or money. This can shape technology trends if Capricorn-led organizations choose carefully and set thoughtful standards.

Business and Corporate Culture

Many companies value Capricorn employees for their reliability. They might be placed in positions that handle complex details or manage schedules. Some Capricorns rise to executive roles because they blend ambition with discipline. They might focus on long-term stability for the company, aiming for slow but steady growth. This can be appealing in an economy that experiences booms and busts.

However, tension can arise if a company's culture wants fast, risky moves while Capricorn urges caution.

Influence in Family Structures

In the home, a Capricorn might become the one who keeps track of monthly bills, organizes important documents, or plans family events. Their relatives may lean on them for guidance in tough times. Extended family members might view them as the stable pillar who can handle crises calmly. Sometimes, this leads to admiration and gratitude. Other times, it can be a burden if everyone expects the Capricorn to fix everything. Capricorns benefit from sharing tasks with others when possible.

Cultural Festivals and Traditions

Across different societies, there might be annual events tied to the zodiac. Some places hold gatherings when the Sun enters Capricorn's segment of the sky. Others might not hold big events but still mention zodiac signs in local traditions. Capricorns might enjoy traditions that honor history or show the passage of time, given their respect for order. They might not always be the ones dancing in the center of the festival, but they could help plan or manage essential details.

Spiritual and Religious Communities

In some spiritual groups, a Capricorn might act as a caretaker of the group's resources or time schedules. They might also handle charitable donations or supplies if the community runs a food drive. Because they appreciate structure, they might help the group follow regular practices. They might not be the loud preacher but could be the one who maintains records or keeps everything organized so that others can focus on spiritual matters. This can make them a vital part of the community's daily flow.

Global Perspective

Looking beyond local society, Capricorns in international roles—like diplomatic missions or global businesses—often excel at long-term planning. They might calmly evaluate economic or cultural differences between countries. Their steady approach can be valuable when forging international agreements. While some global issues require bold changes, a Capricorn's caution might prevent hasty moves that cause bigger problems later. Of course, true diplomacy often blends many viewpoints, so Capricorns must listen to more flexible signs to find a middle ground.

Pop Culture and Memes

In modern pop culture, there are many memes labeling each zodiac sign. Capricorn memes might highlight frugality, discipline, or "workaholic" behavior. They often joke that Capricorn is the "dad" of the zodiac—always the responsible one, scolding others for not following the plan. While these jokes can be funny, they might oversimplify real personalities. Still, a Capricorn might identify with some of them if they have experienced such moments. They might also laugh at how extreme the portrayal is.

Educational Materials and Astrology

There are countless websites, books, and videos discussing zodiac signs. Capricorn is often presented as the sign of maturity. This has trickled into casual conversations, where people say, "You are acting so Capricorn right now," if someone is being no-nonsense. While this can bring mild amusement, it might also create pressure on Capricorns to act "mature" even if they want a more carefree moment. Over time, repeating these ideas might shape how both Capricorns and others see Capricorn traits.

Changing Work Patterns

In today's world, remote work, gig economies, and flexible schedules are more common. Capricorns can adapt by finding systems that keep them on track outside a traditional office. Society's shift away from lifetime employment might unsettle them at first, because they like security. However, many Capricorns discover that if they plan carefully, they can succeed in freelancing or modern work setups. They use their discipline to handle tasks on their own schedule, still meeting deadlines and building a solid reputation.

Challenges in Society for Capricorn

- **Excessive Work Pressure:** Because they are so responsible, Capricorns might feel they must carry a heavier load. Society might see them as capable of more, resulting in burnout.

- **Resistance to Sudden Shifts:** Rapid cultural or technological changes can be stressful for Capricorns if they do not see their long-term value.

- **Undervalued Skills:** Sometimes, people notice flashy or loud talents, overlooking Capricorn's quiet, consistent effort. Capricorns might have to speak up to get credit.

Opportunities for Capricorn Strengths

- **Stable Leadership:** Many organizations seek level-headed managers who do not panic. Capricorns can step in to offer structure.

- **Mentorship Programs:** Capricorns can guide younger or less experienced individuals, teaching them discipline and showing them how to set goals.

- **Community Building:** In local groups or charities, a Capricorn's ability to organize can bring lasting improvements, like well-managed budgets or consistent volunteer scheduling.

Capricorn's Presence in Cultural Works

Musicians, writers, and filmmakers under this sign sometimes create works that show ambition and meticulous detail. For example, a Capricorn author might plan a book's plot thoroughly before writing. A Capricorn composer might refine a piece of music until it meets high standards. Though not all talk about their sign, fans sometimes notice the careful and patient style in their works.

Maintaining Balance in a Fast World

Today's society often demands quick changes. Businesses want immediate results; social media thrives on rapid trends. Capricorns can become overwhelmed if everything moves too fast. Yet, their knack for planning and stable growth is a strength that remains valuable. People who chase quick gains might face burnout, while Capricorn's slow-and-steady mindset can ensure that progress remains consistent. They may also help others by sharing time-management tips or cautioning against impulsive moves.

Respect Earned Over Time

A Capricorn might not get instant applause, but as the months or years go by, people see the solid results of their efforts. This is how Capricorns often gain the respect of a community or workplace. In a culture that sometimes admires instant fame, Capricorn reminds everyone that real success can take time. By patiently building trust and showing reliability, they earn a secure spot in society.

Impact on Future Generations

Because of their focus on planning, Capricorns might pass down lessons about saving, careful decision-making, and long-range thinking. They might show the next generation how to create goals that are reachable. This can influence children or younger members of the community to be more mindful and resourceful. Even if not all kids share the same zodiac sign, they can benefit from Capricorn's experience in creating order and managing resources wisely.

Connecting Across Cultural Borders

In international collaborations, Capricorn's preference for clarity can be an asset. They can draft precise agreements or schedules, reducing confusion among people from different backgrounds. Their calm demeanor can also help resolve cultural misunderstandings by focusing on shared objectives. However, they need to remain aware of diverse communication styles so they do not come across as too rigid or unfeeling.

Social Change and Capricorn's Role

Capricorns might quietly push for improvement in a system. Instead of a loud protest, they could gather facts, build alliances, and present well-crafted proposals to those in authority. This approach can sometimes lead to real, lasting change. While it might lack the drama of huge demonstrations, it can be effective in the long run. If more outspoken signs gain attention, Capricorns may support them by providing structure or statistics that strengthen the cause.

CHAPTER 19: NOTABLE CAPRICORN TALENTS

Understanding Talents vs. Traits

People sometimes confuse natural traits with talents. A trait, such as being organized, is a general way of acting. A talent is a specific skill that a person develops over time. For Capricorn, certain traits—like patience or attention to detail—can guide them toward particular talents. These talents might not be obvious right away. Through practice, they can become areas where Capricorn truly shines. This chapter looks at some common talents that Capricorns may discover and refine, showing how they can turn basic qualities into standout strengths.

Methodical Problem-Solving

One of Capricorn's key talents is the ability to break problems into smaller pieces. This is related to their trait of analyzing details. A Capricorn might see a difficult puzzle—like fixing a broken gadget, planning a big event, or handling an unexpected challenge—and come up with a step-by-step list. This approach can become a true talent when paired with patience. For example, in a job that requires solving complex issues, a Capricorn might become known for thorough solutions that do not miss key steps. Over time, they may refine this skill and become the "go-to" person for tackling tough tasks.

Long-Range Strategy

Many people focus only on what is happening right now. In contrast, Capricorns often think beyond the current moment. When they set out to learn or achieve something, they plan for the future. This can turn into a talent for strategic thinking, whether in a career, personal finances, or group projects. For example, a Capricorn might design a three-year growth plan for a small business or a long-term budget that avoids debt. This talent stands out in teams because many folks get stuck on day-to-day issues, but Capricorn can keep track of bigger goals.

Leadership Through Steadiness

Some leaders attract attention with loud talks or big gestures. Capricorn's style of leadership is different. They bring order by staying calm under pressure, making realistic plans, and following through on promises. This can be a major talent in workplaces or clubs that need stable guidance. Over time, Capricorn may train and manage others with clear rules, ensuring tasks are done properly. Although quiet at times, their leadership can gain respect because they do not panic easily and they rarely abandon the team when problems come up.

Skilled Organization

Another notable talent is the capacity to create effective systems. Whether it is setting up a new filing system at work, arranging schedules for a family, or organizing resources for a neighborhood event, Capricorns often excel at making order. They might enjoy reading about methods or apps that help manage tasks. When they apply these methods, they ensure everything has a place and that steps are clear for everyone involved. This talent can transform a messy or confusing environment into one that runs smoothly.

Careful Communication in Writing

Capricorns often think before they speak, but that same caution can serve them well in writing too. They can be talented at crafting messages, emails, or documents that are concise and clear. Because they do not want to leave room for confusion, they take time to structure their words. For instance, in a company, a Capricorn might be the one who writes the instruction manual because they will check each sentence for clarity. This writing talent can be valuable in many areas—technical writing, blogging about practical tips, or even writing short stories that are well-organized.

Financial Savvy

While not every Capricorn is a money expert, many develop a talent for handling budgets or financial planning. This goes beyond basic saving. They might learn how to compare different saving or investment options, track expenses, and forecast costs for big projects. If they work in accounting or finance, they often stand out for their accuracy. Even in personal life, their knack for money management can help them become a resource for friends who need advice on cutting costs or planning for the future.

Patience in Learning New Skills

Some people dive into a new craft quickly, then drop it when progress slows. Capricorn's steady mindset can become a real talent for mastery. Whether it is learning a musical instrument, practicing a craft, or studying a foreign language, Capricorns tend to keep going, even if they only improve a bit each day. Their patience is an advantage. After a year or two, they might look back and see impressive progress, while those who wanted instant results have long given up. This calm, methodical learning style can turn many interests into true abilities.

Reliability as a Team Player

Sometimes, reliability is overlooked as a talent. But it can be very special, especially in group work. Knowing that a Capricorn will keep track of deadlines, complete tasks, and do them well can be a huge relief to others. Over time, this builds a reputation that can open doors—people want Capricorn on their team because they can trust the outcome. This talent may not look flashy, but it has real power to bring stability and success to collective efforts.

Technical or Mechanical Aptitude

Because Capricorns like solving problems step by step, they can grow talented at fixing or building things. For example, in a technical job—like engineering, coding, or mechanics—they might figure out how systems fit together. They break tasks into smaller bits, test each part, and fix errors patiently. Others might become frustrated when something is not working, but Capricorn keeps going until they spot the root cause. This methodical approach can help them master complicated tools, software, or machines.

Calm Mediation and Conflict Resolution

Disagreements happen in any group. A Capricorn's cool-headed nature can be a talent when guiding people through conflicts. They can ask each side to share facts, then look for a fair solution that works for everyone. Because they avoid loud drama and focus on what will solve the problem, they can calm heated situations. This might be a talent in a family setting, a community board, or a professional environment. People often trust Capricorn to handle disputes because they do not ignore facts, and they do not let emotions take over.

Self-Discipline in Fitness or Hobbies

Some Capricorns use their discipline to stay consistent with health routines or personal interests. They might become skilled at a particular sport, practicing the fundamentals carefully each day. Or they might follow a set schedule for painting, coding, or cooking. Because they see small gains add up over time, they do not mind repeating steps to improve. This self-discipline can turn an average interest into a strong skill. Others may wonder how Capricorn sticks to it, but for Capricorn, it feels natural to keep going, one step at a time.

Advising Others with Practical Tips

Friends or family might turn to a Capricorn for straightforward advice. This can become a talent in consulting, coaching, or guiding people in personal decisions. They may not use flowery words, but they offer realistic options. For example, if someone is unsure about a career move, Capricorn might help them outline pros and cons, check the finances, and plan a safe approach. If a friend needs a study routine, Capricorn can break down the schedule. Over time, these practical tips can greatly help people achieve goals without unnecessary risks.

Attention to Quality and Detail

Quality control is another area where Capricorns can excel. They notice small things that others skip—like a slight mismatch in a design, a tiny bug in a code, or a missing piece in a puzzle. They might also test items or processes carefully to ensure they meet a high standard. In business, this can translate into a quality assurance role, where the Capricorn reviews products before they ship. At home, it might mean that Capricorn is the one who always spots and fixes minor issues, maintaining a high level of excellence in what they do.

Presentation Skills through Preparation

While some signs might win a crowd with showy performance, Capricorn's presentation talent rests on preparation. They research their topic, create solid outlines, and practice until they feel confident. This allows them to deliver speeches or run meetings without stumbling. They may speak in a calm, measured voice, focusing on facts. Though it might not have the same flash as a more theatrical style, it can be very effective in professional settings or educational talks. Audiences often come away trusting the Capricorn's points because they are so well-prepared.

Mentoring and Apprenticeship

Capricorns often do well as mentors or trainers because they can teach in a methodical way. They might design step-by-step lessons for a new coworker or an apprentice. If the learner is willing, they will pass on best practices, correct small mistakes early, and guide them toward independence. This process takes patience, which suits Capricorn. Over time, they might become a respected guide in their field, known for producing capable, well-trained learners.

Transforming Challenges into Skills

Capricorns might encounter an area of weakness—perhaps public speaking or dealing with emotional topics—and decide to master it. They use their determination and research skills to break down the challenge. For instance, if they dislike talking in front of groups, they might read about techniques, practice in front of a mirror, and gradually speak to small audiences. Over months or years, they can turn that past difficulty into a surprising talent, showing how their methodical approach can reshape personal limitations.

Planning Successful Events

Whether it is a birthday gathering, a team-building retreat, or a community fundraiser, Capricorns often excel at event planning. They set a timeline, assign tasks, and manage budgets. They might create checklists for decorations, food, and activities. By double-checking details, they reduce the chance of last-minute mishaps. This talent can make them the person everyone calls when an organized event is needed. While they may not crave the spotlight at the event, they find satisfaction in seeing it run smoothly.

Developing Strong Professional Reputations

Many Capricorns become known in their field for trustworthiness and thoroughness. Over time, this reputation is a talent on its own—people know they can rely on the Capricorn. This can open up top-level work offers or collaborations. They might not jump from job to job quickly, but each role builds a track record. Because they rarely burn bridges or leave chaos behind, their name grows in a positive way. This intangible "talent for reliability" can be a big asset in the long run.

Combining Logic with Sensitivity

While Capricorn is seen as logical, many develop a talent for reading people's unspoken signals. They might notice subtle signs of stress in a coworker or sense tension between family members. Their calm logic can then lead them to offer helpful solutions without turning it into a big scene. This balanced mix of reason and quiet empathy can become a special talent for guiding groups or supporting loved ones who are upset.

Steady Dedication to Personal Projects

Not all talents show up in jobs. Capricorn might discover a personal hobby—like woodworking, gardening, or an online channel—where they invest time outside of work. Their steady approach can help them produce high-quality results, even if progress is slow. They might become known among friends for these side projects. Though it is not their main career, the care they show in perfecting details can spark admiration and personal pride.

Thriving in Structured Roles

Some fields have strict guidelines or systems to follow—like insurance, programming, or supply chain management. Capricorns can rise to the top in these areas because they appreciate rules that keep order. They turn the guidelines into a personal system, continuing to refine how tasks are done. Over time, they might suggest improvements that help the entire department. This is where their organized mind truly shows its worth, becoming a notable talent that benefits the broader team.

Adapting Capricorn Talents Over Time

Talents are not fixed. A Capricorn might start with a knack for budgeting, then grow into a full financial advisor over the years. Or they might begin with small leadership tasks, gradually taking on bigger roles. Each life phase can shape how their talents evolve. In older adulthood, they might shift from active leadership to mentoring, passing down their carefully learned skills. The key is that they keep using their discipline and curiosity to refine what they can do.

Sharing Talents with Others

It is not uncommon for Capricorn to keep certain abilities to themselves, especially if they do not want to brag. Yet sharing these talents can benefit friends, family, or coworkers. Offering to teach, help, or guide can create a supportive environment. It also reinforces the Capricorn's own skill, since teaching often deepens understanding. Over time, they can develop a sense of fulfillment from seeing others grow thanks to what they shared.

Building Confidence Through Small Wins

Since some Capricorns worry about perfection, they might doubt their own talents. The best way to handle that is by taking on projects that match their skills, completing them with care, and noticing each success. Small wins—like organizing a community event or solving a tricky software bug—add up. Each victory confirms that their steady method works. This builds confidence, which in turn encourages them to aim for bigger tasks. Over time, their talents become more visible, both to themselves and to those around them.

Staying Open to New Methods

A Capricorn's strong sense of structure can sometimes lock them into old ways of doing things. But real talent often grows when fresh ideas are considered. For instance, if a Capricorn is an excellent event planner, they might explore new digital platforms for invitations or scheduling. If they are skilled at finances, they might study modern approaches to investing. Staying open to change can keep their talents relevant and let them discover better strategies they might have missed otherwise.

Handling Setbacks While Developing Talents

Even with natural gifts, setbacks happen. A Capricorn might face a project that fails, a rejected proposal, or a skill that proves harder than expected. Their advantage is their willingness to regroup and try again. This perseverance can turn a minor defeat into a lesson that sharpens their talents. By calmly assessing what went wrong, they can avoid repeating errors. Over time, these mistakes can lead to advanced abilities that do not crumble in tough conditions.

Celebrating Talents in a Modest Way

Some people show off their talents openly. Capricorns often take a more modest path. They might let results speak for themselves rather than announcing their abilities. However, a bit of self-recognition is healthy. A Capricorn can quietly acknowledge, "I did a good job with this, and it took effort." This helps them avoid feeling unappreciated or unseen. Sharing updates or achievements with trusted friends or mentors can also bring encouragement that fuels further development.

CHAPTER 20: LOOKING AHEAD FOR CAPRICORN

Why Look to the Future?

Capricorns place value on planning and stability, which naturally leads them to wonder what lies ahead. Shifts in technology, workplace patterns, and social structures can alter life's path for everyone, including those with a cautious approach. By considering upcoming trends and possible changes, Capricorns can prepare themselves to remain steady while also embracing beneficial adaptations. This chapter offers thoughts on how Capricorns might continue to grow, find fulfillment, and maintain calm in a world that seems to change faster every day.

Adapting to Rapid Technological Changes

Technology is likely to keep moving ahead quickly—more remote work, new apps, and automation. For Capricorns, it may be tempting to stick with older methods if they feel secure. Yet staying relevant means exploring these tools in a measured way. A Capricorn can research a new tool, run a test, and gradually bring it into their routine. This lets them keep their sense of control while not ignoring the value of modern solutions. Over time, they can become guides for others, showing how to use new tech logically rather than rushing blindly.

Balancing Stability with Innovation

Capricorn's preference for safety does not have to prevent them from trying new ideas. The future may reward those who dare to combine proven methods with creative thinking. For instance, a Capricorn in management might adopt an innovative training program that breaks from old patterns, but still test it in small steps first. This blend of caution and openness can help them excel in fields that are evolving. By approaching changes systematically, they can remain the steady voice in a changing environment, but also reap the benefits of progress.

Growth in Remote and Flexible Work

Many jobs now allow people to work outside a traditional office or on their own schedule. Capricorns can thrive in such settings if they design a clear structure for themselves. For example, they can set a daily work timetable at home and keep a well-organized workspace. Their discipline helps them avoid distractions. As remote work becomes more common, Capricorns can use their planning strengths to remain productive while also enjoying more personal flexibility. They might find that this arrangement allows them to handle personal responsibilities or hobbies without losing work quality.

International Opportunities

A fast-changing world also means more global connections. Capricorns might consider careers or projects that link them with different countries. Their approach to order and consistency can be valuable in cross-cultural teams that need a steady framework. Learning a new language or studying global business methods can open fresh doors. While stepping outside their usual comfort zone, Capricorns can still use their structured mindset to handle complexities, becoming valuable team members or leaders in multinational groups.

Coping with Social and Cultural Shifts

Societies are experiencing new debates—ranging from environmental concerns to social changes. Capricorns, with their sense of duty, can be part of finding grounded solutions. They might get involved in local planning for recycling or efficient energy use, for example. Their reliable nature can help communities adopt changes that make sense. Instead of ignoring these shifts, Capricorns might see them as chances to strengthen systems. By thinking about the long-term impact, they can steer efforts in a practical, sustainable direction.

Personal Life Stages Ahead

As Capricorns move through their 30s, 40s, and beyond, they often discover new priorities. They might have built a career and now want to focus on family, or they might want more personal fulfillment after years of hard effort. The future could bring a desire to slow down or explore new passions that do not link directly to work. Whether it is traveling in a measured way or taking up a creative hobby, Capricorns can plan these transitions so they do not feel abrupt. By pacing themselves, they stay calm and enjoy new chapters of life without losing their sense of structure.

Deepening Emotional Connections

Over time, many Capricorns realize that strong bonds with friends, partners, and children matter as much as professional goals. The future can include more shared moments, from family dinners to weekend outings, if Capricorns schedule them in just as they schedule other tasks. This allows them to express care without feeling off-balance. By allocating time for emotional closeness, they can keep a stable personal life. This, in turn, brings satisfaction that purely work-focused living might miss.

New Avenues for Learning

Continuous learning is crucial in a fast-paced world. Capricorns already have patience for study, so looking ahead might involve picking a fresh topic or a new skill every few years. This could mean online courses, workshops, or returning to school for advanced certificates. Because they excel at planning, Capricorns can fit these learning steps around their current responsibilities. Each new skill can prepare them for roles or interests that arise, ensuring they do not feel left behind as industries evolve.

Legacy and Long-Term Impact

Many Capricorns think about how they will be remembered. They might wonder: "What am I building that will last?" Looking ahead, this might involve mentoring younger people, writing about their experiences, or creating a project that benefits the next generation. For instance, a Capricorn could help set up scholarship funds, advise new business owners, or guide community development. Such actions align with their desire for stability and offer a sense of purpose beyond their own lifetime.

Handling Environmental Concerns

With ecological issues on the rise, there is a growing push for practical solutions. Capricorns can bring logic and organization to environmental projects, whether that is working on local clean-ups, supporting renewable energy, or planning community gardens. They might not lead big protests, but their knack for slow, steady improvement can make these efforts more effective. Over the years, such involvement can help them connect with like-minded people who also value responsible management of resources.

Financial Future and Security

With economic ups and downs expected, Capricorns might double down on careful financial planning. They may split funds into stable and moderate-risk investments to protect themselves. They might also teach younger family members about money basics. Knowing they have a financial cushion helps Capricorns explore new paths without too much worry. Whether the future brings short downturns or big shifts in job markets, their well-crafted savings plan can keep them on steady ground.

Embracing Health and Wellness

As the future unfolds, health research is likely to keep evolving. Capricorns who pay attention to new findings can adapt their routines in sensible ways—perhaps adding moderate exercises proven to boost heart health or trying balanced diets that experts recommend. Because Capricorns are good at following structured programs, they can manage their health effectively. This might mean scheduling regular checkups, tracking simple metrics (like steps walked per day), or finding a relaxing hobby that lowers stress. Looking ahead, prioritizing both mental and physical well-being helps them remain energetic and able to meet life's demands.

Flexible Retirement Plans

Traditional retirements are changing. Some people retire later, switch to part-time, or start small businesses in their later years. Capricorns, who appreciate being productive, might choose a flexible retirement where they continue working a little, consulting, or focusing on personal projects. They can plan for this by gradually cutting back hours, transferring duties, or training a successor. This approach lets them remain active while still enjoying more free time. Because they tend to manage resources carefully, many Capricorns can craft a retirement that fits their sense of order.

Exploring Inner Passions

Not all of Capricorn's future plans need to revolve around outward success. They might find themselves drawn to creative arts, spiritual practices, or adventures that feed the soul. For example, a Capricorn might take up painting classes after work or join a meditation group. Initially, they could be unsure if this is a good "use" of time. But as they see emotional and mental benefits, they realize it is an investment in their personal happiness. Letting themselves try new pastimes can open fresh horizons they never considered when younger.

Incorporating Community Leadership

In many towns and cities, local boards and committees need responsible folks to guide planning for parks, libraries, or neighborhood safety. Capricorns might step into such roles. Their organized approach can ensure that community funds are spent wisely, and that projects stay on schedule. Over the years, they might become recognized figures who keep local initiatives on track. This can be a satisfying way to give back, blending a Capricorn's sense of duty with visible results.

Growth in Emotional Intelligence

The future often prizes not just practical skills but also emotional understanding. Capricorns who develop empathy and emotional awareness can handle complicated relationships better. They might practice listening without rushing to fix everything, giving space for people's feelings, and offering gentle support. While logic remains their strength, adding genuine warmth can improve teamwork and personal bonds. This balanced style can help them stand out as both capable and caring, an appealing mix in many environments.

Maintaining Boundaries in an Always-Connected World

Modern life can blur the line between work and rest, especially with constant notifications. Capricorns may need to decide when to switch off. Scheduling time away from devices or turning off work emails after certain hours helps protect mental health. Because they value order, Capricorns can turn these offline moments into part of their regular schedule. This keeps them from feeling overwhelmed or always "on call," which can happen more often in the future as technology advances.

Supporting Younger Generations

Younger people may face new challenges that did not exist before—like digital overload or fierce job competition. A Capricorn can use their experience to guide them. They might mentor interns, help nieces or nephews learn budgeting, or create resources for new graduates. By encouraging steady progress and showing how to break down big goals, Capricorns can help younger folks develop confidence and clarity. Looking ahead, this type of guidance can shape the next wave of determined, practical individuals.

Stepping Beyond Comfort Zones

While it is good for Capricorn to stick to what works, the future might bring times when trying something new is valuable. They could consider traveling to unfamiliar places or collaborating with people from different backgrounds. Even if they plan thoroughly, they might encounter situations where quick flexibility is needed. By practicing adaptability, they become even more resilient. This does not mean dropping all caution, but learning to see new or surprising paths as possible growth opportunities instead of immediate risks.

Staying True to Core Values

Even as they explore new trends, Capricorns hold certain timeless values: honesty, hard effort, loyalty, and fairness. The future can challenge these values if shortcuts or questionable actions become tempting. But by staying faithful to what they believe, Capricorns can remain respected. Over the long run, people often turn to those with integrity. So, if Capricorns stay consistent while allowing sensible updates to their methods, they can keep a strong moral center in an ever-shifting world.

Finding Mentors for the Next Steps

Nobody is too old or experienced to benefit from mentors. A Capricorn heading into new territory—like advanced technology or a different career track—might seek mentors who have already walked that path. While Capricorns are known for self-reliance, outside advice can speed up learning. These mentors might come from different generations or fields, offering fresh viewpoints. By blending outside wisdom with their own organized approach, Capricorns set themselves up for more success and fewer errors.

Facing Uncertainty with Steady Resolve

The future is uncertain: economic changes, shifts in job demands, and unexpected global events can happen. Capricorns, however, are well-prepared if they keep a balanced view. They might maintain an emergency fund, keep learning, and watch for signs that a field is becoming outdated. Their calm manner can reassure families and coworkers during crises. Although they cannot see every surprise coming, their flexible planning method helps them pivot without panic. By staying focused on what they can control, Capricorns reduce the anxiety of change.

Embracing a Legacy of Guidance

Eventually, many Capricorns reach a point where they want to pass on what they have built. They might sell a business, let a younger partner step up, or shift their role in a community. This process can be smoother if they plan for it. They can train successors or create clear instructions. This final stage can bring peace of mind, knowing their work will live on. It also frees them to explore personal hobbies or enjoy a simpler routine, trusting that they have left stable foundations behind.

Opportunities for Personal Reinvention

Looking ahead, Capricorns do not have to keep the same identity forever. If a Capricorn originally defined themselves by their job, they might branch out into volunteer work or a personal passion. If they spent early years focusing on money, they may devote later years to travel or writing. The point is, they have the power to reinvent parts of their life if they choose. Because they have strong planning skills, they can explore new directions securely, ensuring they keep a safety net in place.

Building a Balanced Future

Balance is key: a mix of caution and openness, of tradition and progress, and of work and personal life. By looking ahead carefully, Capricorns can remain grounded but not stagnant. They can find ways to serve others while also feeding their own growth. This balanced viewpoint ensures they do not miss out on life's joys or become so rigid that they cannot adapt.

Sharing Hope and Stability

In uncertain times, people often look for steady figures who do not bend in the wind. A Capricorn with a well-planned outlook can become that anchor. By staying calm and showing that solutions are possible—even if they are not instant—they encourage others to keep going. Whether through community roles, leadership at work, or simple friendship, Capricorns can spread a sense of hope and practicality, reminding people that steady effort makes a difference.

Concluding Thoughts on the Road Ahead

The future holds many possibilities for Capricorns, from new career models to changing family structures. By leaning on their natural skills—like planning, patience, and focus—they can find paths that suit their values. They do not have to fear technology or social change if they approach both with methodical care. In their personal lives, they can grow emotionally, learning to open up while keeping their love for order. Through it all, they remain the reliable foundation that others trust. By balancing caution with a willingness to learn, Capricorns can look ahead with confidence, ready to shape a meaningful future for themselves and those around them.

Final Reflections

Throughout this book, we have seen how Capricorn's careful spirit touches every area of life. That same spirit can guide them into the coming years. Their steady, reliable style may not always grab headlines, but it continues to earn deep respect. With each new step, Capricorns can draw on their strengths—such as discipline, moral backbone, and loyalty—to find opportunities and adapt to whatever changes lie ahead. As they do, they remain a stabilizing force in a world that sometimes forgets the power of consistent, well-planned progress.

Help Us Share Your Thoughts!

Dear reader,

Thank you for spending your time with this book. We hope it brought you enjoyment and a few new ideas to think about. If there was anything that didn't work for you, or if you have suggestions on how we can improve, please let us know at **kontakt@skriuwer.com**. Your feedback means a lot to us and helps us make our books even better.

If you enjoyed this book, we would be very grateful if you left a review on the site where you purchased it. Your review not only helps other readers find our books, but also encourages us to keep creating more stories and materials that you'll love.

By choosing Skriuwer, you're also supporting **Frisian**—a minority language mainly spoken in the northern Netherlands. Although **Frisian** has a rich history, the number of speakers is shrinking, and it's at risk of dying out. Your purchase helps fund resources to preserve and promote this language, such as educational programs and learning tools. If you'd like to learn more about Frisian or even start learning it yourself, please visit **www.learnfrisian.com**.

Thank you for being part of our community. We look forward to sharing more books with you in the future.

Warm regards,
The Skriuwer Team